UNDER THE BRIGHT WINGS

Peter Harris

Illustrations by
Susan Rubira

REGENT COLLEGE PUBLISHING
· VANCOUVER, BRITISH COLUMBIA ·

Under the Bright Wings
Copyright © 1993 Peter Harris

First published 1993 in Great Britain by
Hodder & Stoughton
A division of Hodder Headline PLC
338 Euston Road
London NW1 3BH U.K.

Reprinted 2000 by Regent College Publishing
5800 University Blvd., Vancouver, BC V6T 2E4 Canada
www.regentpublishing.com

Views expressed in works published by
Regent College Publishing
are those of the author and do not necessarily
represent the official position of Regent College.

Printed in the United States of America

Canadian Cataloguing in Publication Data

Harris, Peter, 1952–

ISBN 0-88865-697-1 (Canada)
ISBN 1-57383-188-3 (U.S.A.)

1. Harris, Peter, 1952– 2. Harris, Miranda.
3. A Rocha Christian Field Study Centre and Bird Observatory.
4. Human ecology—Religious aspects—Christianity.
5. Birds—Religious aspects—Christianity.
6. Environmental ethics. 1. Title

BT695.5.H37 2000   261.8'362   C00-910912-9

And for all this, nature is never spent;
There lives the dearest freshness deep down things;
And though the last lights off the black West went
Oh, morning, at the brown brink eastward, springs –
Because the Holy Ghost over the bent
World broods with warm breast and with ah! bright wings.

"God's Grandeur", Gerard Manley Hopkins

Acknowledgments

"Books are best written in community," said Richard Foster, and I would agree; this book has certainly been a communal effort. Without the love and courage of my wife Miranda there would have been no community to write about, and much of what I have written would have been even more incoherent without her patient attention. I also want to thank Joanna, Esther, Jeremy and Bethan for putting up with a preoccupied father, and for occasionally not putting up with it, which was usually more fun.

The other members of the current A Rocha team were happy to cover my reluctant retreat from much that went on at Cruzinha last winter, so thank you Colin, Will, Rosário and Paula.

As will be apparent from the following pages, A Rocha owes its continuing existence to the efforts of a large number of people, and I wish to thank the A Rocha Trustees, particularly Bob Pullan and Alan Coverdale, and John Ball at Crosslinks, for their perseverance and belief over the last ten years. It would take another book to begin to thank all the many others I cannot name here for the many and varied gifts they have uncomplainingly brought to their work for A Rocha, either in Portugal or the UK. To protect places and people I have changed some names.

Both Miranda and I owe more than we can easily say to our parents who have given us and A Rocha their affirmation and support in countless different ways.

I am grateful to Ruth Goring Stewart for permission to recycle one of the chapter headings from her booklet, *Environmental Stewardship* (IVP), as the title of this book.

Finally I want to thank Susan Rubira for the wonderfully evocative drawings and a beautiful cover, and Carolyn Armitage at Hodder and Stoughton whose commitment to this book and patience with the limitations of its author were a constant encouragement.

Foreword

Peter Harris is an Englishman who, being both clergyman and ornithologist, has founded a field centre in Portugal in the interests of conservation and evangelism.

Under the Bright Wings is his personal story of the last nine years in the Algarve, told with modesty, passion and charm, and interspersed with insightful theological reflection on the environmental debate.

Peter refuses to compartmentalise Christian discipleship. His overriding concern is to help break down the disastrous dualism which still exists in many Christians between the sacred and the secular, the spiritual and the material, the soul and the body, as if God were interested only in the former, in the "religious" bits of our lives, and as if only they deserve to be called "Christian".

But the living God of the Bible is the God of both creation and redemption, and is concerned for the totality of our well-being. Put another way, the older theologians used to say that God has written two books, one called "nature" and the other called "Scripture", through which he has revealed himself. Moreover, he has given us these two books to study. The study of the natural order is "science", and of the biblical revelation "theology". And as we engage in these twin disciplines, we are (in the words of the seventeenth-century astronomer Johann Kepler) "thinking God's thoughts after him".

Christian people should surely have been in the vanguard of the movement for environmental responsibility, because of our doctrines of creation and stewardship. Did God make the world? Does he sustain it? Has he committed its resources to our care? His personal concern for his own creation should be sufficient to inspire us to be equally concerned.

But can ecological involvement properly be included under the heading of "mission"? Yes, it can and should. For mission embraces everything Christ sends his people into the world to do, service as well as evangelism. And we cannot truly love and serve our neighbours if at the same time we are destroying their environment, or acquiescing in its destruction, or even ignoring the environmentally depleted circumstances in which so many people are condemned to live. As by the incarnation Jesus Christ entered into our world, so true incarnational mission involves entering into other people's worlds, including the world of their social and environmental reality.

The gospel itself includes God's creation as well as his work of redemption. Certainly the apostle Paul, in his sermon to the Athenian philosophers, ranged much more widely than we usually do in our gospel preaching. He took in the whole of time from the creation to the consummation, and demonstrated from the truth of God as creator and sustainer of all things the sheer absurdity of worshipping idols made by human hands.

As for methods of evangelism, an activity which Peter Harris clearly and rightly distinguishes from both propaganda and proselytism, he lays his emphasis on the importance of the Christian community. Of course the gospel must be articulated in words. But so deeply alienated are contemporary Europeans from the traditional image of the church, that almost nothing is more important than that people should be able to *see* what we are talking about. In consequence, Peter and Miranda and their four children have opened their hearts and their home to people. They welcome virtually everybody who comes. It has been a costly commitment. The pressures have been relentless. And they recognise that there must be sensible limits to this kind of exposure. Nevertheless, they are determined that the gospel of God's love will be given visible and tangible expression at Cruzinha.

Peter's account of the A Rocha odyssey is marked both by humility (although the centre has already had a remarkable influence on the conservation movement in Portugal) and by honesty (he neither exaggerates, nor portrays himself, his family and his colleagues as other than flawed and frail human beings). At times his narrative is also hilariously funny, as he laughs at the vagaries of the human scene and at himself. I hope many people will read his book. They are sure to be enriched by it.

It will be evident to readers that I love and admire Peter and Miranda, and enormously enjoyed a recent birdwatching expedition with them in north-west Turkey, as I had also enjoyed some previous birding with Peter in Portugal, west Wales and Morocco. I thank God for their vision, commitment, faith and perseverance, their love for the people they are seeking to serve, and their deep immersion in the Portuguese language and culture. In the developing ministry of A Rocha an exciting, contemporary form of Christian mission has come alive.

JOHN STOTT,
July 1992

1

"... known-land, known-shore, home-shore, home-light." – David Jones

We have been living on the edge of a small village in the south of Portugal for over nine years now. Sometimes, in the stress of the irregular hours and eccentric episodes that make up life in a field study centre and bird observatory we ask ourselves how it all began, simply to find a culprit. My wife Miranda would not describe herself as a fanatical birder, and so she finds it trying if she has invited friends to supper and discovers that everyone has disappeared to watch an owl being ringed in the common room downstairs just as the food gets to the table. For my part, I am strictly a birder and so don't enjoy finding snakes in the fridge, put there by an over-enthusiastic photographer "to slow them down a bit", or giving up the freezer to the corpse of a fox until a budding taxidermist has had time to deal with it. Come to that, neither of us has grown particularly fond of the Portuguese student penchant for arriving at one or two in the morning.

But at other times, when we hear that our field work has helped to save a small piece of nearby marshland from being drained and developed, or when we walk out through the almond orchards on a Sunday morning with the children and they say that they want to live here forever, we remember with more gratitude how it all came about.

It is somehow typical of our rather disorganised life that it

1

all began casually and inconsequentially. At the time we were working in a parish on Merseyside where I was the curate. Our three children, Joanna, Esther and Jeremy, were still small, although the girls were old enough to sound reasonably scouse when it suited them. On days off I used to get out when I could to watch birds on the Mersey, particularly to photograph gulls for a book that was being produced at the time. This was not without its challenges for all the family, not least because it was necessary to black out the bathroom for some hours to develop the pictures. Inevitably the phone would go with news of a particularly pressing pastoral crisis just as I had the hopelessly Heath Robinson blackout apparatus in place, and the first paper in the chemicals. Probably only a birder will appreciate the true moral difficulties of one occasion when there was a choice between printing crisp images of a Sabine's Gull, normally seen on the Mersey only once a year at the most, and helping to bring a marriage back from the brink. In the event I chose to abandon the photo for another six weeks, or perhaps I wouldn't be telling the story.

I had always had a serious interest in birding, but life in a busy church with a small family didn't leave us much time. Some years before, we had decided not to look for work in nature conservation, but to give our full energies to what we then understood as "full-time Christian work". When we eventually found a curacy in a built-up area, I had seen it as a symbolic and slightly heroic renunciation. We were not to know that despite being decidedly urban, Merseyside would offer plenty of ornithological distractions. Heavy autumn gales brought high numbers of seabirds to the nearby shore just as the church programme was at its busiest. It was a scramble to get to team prayers at eight thirty in the morning after a dawn foray to watch an impressive migration of finches at the estuary four miles away. Muddy wellington boots and a heavy Icelandic sweater do not feature in the usual liturgical kit-list.

I can remember one afternoon when I was talking to a lonely and housebound lady who had become quite a friend in the weeks that I had been calling in. We were deep in conversation when my eyes strayed to the lawn that was just visible over her left shoulder and I noticed a Brambling feeding among the customary flock of Chaffinches. Very few had been seen in the area that winter, but I suspected that she wouldn't feel it was quite the consolation she was looking for. "Cheer up, there's a Brambling on your lawn" wasn't one of the recognised punch-lines in the counselling manuals we had been given at theological college. Fortunately it soon went out of range of my surreptitious glances. Despite these tricky moments, God did not seem to be entirely lining up on the expected side of the conflict. The deep feeling for wildlife and its protection seemed to flourish as our understanding of the character of God began to deepen in the stress of pastoral crises and an over-busy home life. In fact the conflict itself appeared to be disappearing. The challenge was what to make of it all.

Working on the gull photos, and meeting birders in the area, led to the idea of organising an expedition to watch birds in southern Sweden. The aim of the trip, which was for students doing environmentally related courses of some kind, was to explore the biblical teaching on the natural world in the context of some practical field work. For many students, the only Christian teaching that they heard on Creation had to do with the contentious issue of its origins. There was little interest in the environment or concern about the present disasters overtaking the world that Christians believed God had made. Even the word Creation had become difficult to use in its plain sense because heated debate had so coloured its meaning. As a friend pointed out, this was rather like seeing a man fall off the back of a boat, and everyone on board arguing about how he had fallen in, rather than throwing him a lifebelt. Anyway, there was something pleasantly eccentric about the presence of an ornithological trip in the list of more orthodox activities that the Universities and Colleges Christian Fellowship were sponsoring that year.

So it was that in the fading heat of a Scandinavian autumn afternoon a group of us were lying on the heather watching hundreds of Honey Buzzards circling in the thermals overhead, gaining height before attempting the narrow Baltic

3

crossing to Germany. On other days bad weather had kept us in the tents, but today conditions had been perfect and we had witnessed one of the great spectacles of migration as thousands of birds of prey poured southwards out of Sweden to escape the coming winter. We were beginning to relax after all the counting, and the conversation turned to future plans.

Most of the group were returning to college, but a zoologist called Les Batty who had joined the expedition at the last minute began talking about his hopes to establish a Christian field study centre somewhere in the north of England. Since Miranda and I had stayed at the bird observatory on the Welsh island of Skokholm some years before (a venture she chiefly remembers for being five months pregnant and halfway down a cliff to the boat when she was handed a huge box of groceries and told in no uncertain terms not to drop it – but that's another story) we had often thought that there would be great possibilities for a place like that run by Christians. Away from the television, and out on top of the superb Welsh cliffs with seabirds all around and carpets of thrift and campion making the air fragrant, people seemed to have space to think and to

talk in a way that they could rarely do when they were surrounded by the normal distractions of their lives.

Such a response to being out on the cliffs isn't surprising,
because the natural world was created, in part at least, to give
exactly that kind of prompting; to make us consider if there
might be a God and, if so, what he might be like. The world
around is studded with clues, even if some of them are hard
to comprehend. In a bird observatory such as Skokholm, the
day ends around a common meal with good conversation and
time to reflect on all that has been seen by everyone staying.
If all of that could be enriched by Christian hospitality and
care, what a wonderful place could be imagined. Nevertheless
we had never expected that it could be more than a good idea,
and on that afternoon in Sweden I wasn't entirely serious when
I asked Les if he might welcome some help.

We had already started to make enquiries about going to
work in the Third World when we finished working in Upton,
and had committed ourselves to an Anglican missionary
society with the honourable but unwieldy name of the Bible
Churchman's Missionary Society (now changed to Crosslinks).
It had been suggested that we might go to Tanzania, perhaps
to pastor a church and to help with theological education.
Despite the stubborn and awkward pull towards nature protection, we had set our course and there seemed to be little we
could do to alter it.

I've learnt since that Les doesn't recognise the obstacles that
many other people do, and so we continued to talk about the
idea later that day.

"Where exactly are you planning to open this centre of
yours, Les?"

"Probably in the north-east, perhaps the Northumberland
coast. We're still looking for a place."

"Pity about that. Not that it is isn't a wonderful area, but it's
just that there are a lot of field centres in the UK already, and
not many in the south of Europe. Ditto committed Christians.
Ever thought of Portugal?"

Now I have to admit that this was a little devious. Since
student days when I had seen something of the struggles of

tiny churches in Asia, I had had an unsophisticated conviction that it was better to spend your life where Christian resources were limited. Miranda had belonged for a year to a small fellowship in France, and had helped with a project in Morocco during one of her student vacations, and so she was equally keen to work outside the UK where Christian organisations seem relatively well off. So if we were ever going to be involved we would be looking for somewhere off the beaten church track. A project like this would have to be in Europe, and the only place in Europe where I knew BCMS had some workers was Portugal. Somewhat to my surprise, Les was very positive and confident that Wendy, his wife, would be happy to alter her plans to live in north-east England for the unknown in Portugal.

At that stage all we knew of Portugal that seemed relevant was that both its nature conservation organisations and its churches were struggling. We had heard of the well-known problems that mass tourism had brought to the fragile habitats in the Mediterranean area, and had read of the trapping and shooting of millions of bird migrants. But even though we knew there was an invitation for a clergyman to go and help the Anglican church, the Igreja Lusitana, it seemed unlikely that they would consider nature conservation as being an appropriate contribution.

However, when I got back home and talked to Miranda, she was immediately very enthusiastic. We both had a strange and sudden conviction that after some months of having very little certainty about the plans we were making for when we left the parish, this might just be the direction we should take. The number of times we had experienced such convictions could be numbered on the fingers of one hand, and we were all the more wary because on at least one previous occasion we had been completely wrong, but we shared an undeniable intuition that something was going on. If this intuition was correct, we felt it could be entrusted to God to bring it about and so we resolved not to question our commitment to go to Tanzania until it should prove impossible. We prayed that night, and then agreed to do nothing. (Incidentally, the truth

about us is that we don't pray together nearly enough, but when we do, we always realise that we should do more. Does that sound familiar?) We hadn't heard from BCMS for about five months by then, but the next morning there was a letter from their general secretary, John Ball:

> I am sure you will be wondering whether I have any definite news for you about the future. I am only too sorry to tell you that at the moment I do not have anything definite. I had a long talk with Bishop Alpha of the Diocese of Mount Kilimanjaro, but ... it seems there may be other plans for the way he wants things to develop in the diocese.

The timing of the letter seemed uncomfortably precise. Now it came to it, I didn't find it easy to relinquish the hopes that we had cherished for many years of working in Africa. The reality of staying in Europe seemed very mundane given the desperate needs of so many places in the Third World. But it all looked ominously like the leading from God that we had asked for.

It transpired that John was to be in Liverpool the following weekend, so we agreed to meet. Over a two-hour cup of tea we explained what we were beginning to think about. He had just produced a paper outlining the way he hoped BCMS would develop and which was to guide its approach to mission in the next few years, and he was keen to bring in a new emphasis on the international nature of the church and a wholehearted involvement in society.

"This is like a hand in a glove," he said. "A project like this exactly fits in to the new direction that we are taking. More than that, a member of the church I led in Nairobi was a director of the Kenya Wildlife Service, and we often talked about the need for Christian thinking and action on environmental issues."

So it was that John understood immediately what we were talking about, and from that moment his support has never wavered. While no one else had considered the environment as being relevant to mission so far, he encouraged us to explore the idea further. He warned us that it was unlikely that BCMS could take on the project themselves; quite apart from anything else they wouldn't wish to get into the business of owning property overseas. If we could establish a charitable trust, however, then they could second us to the trust, but the next step was to sound out the Igreja Lusitana.

Much-maligned Merseyside is not renowned for the beauty of its sunsets, but that evening in October there was a real classic, and as we drove back towards the Mersey tunnel into the blazing orange sky ahead of us, it all seemed a little unreal. Had we really heard the general secretary of a mainstream Anglican missionary society say he could quite understand that bird protection and study were well worth doing as mission? Were we really going to be able to try out all the ideas that had been brewing for what seemed like quite a while by now?

8

After the years of resolutely putting all hopes of working in conservation on one side, it hardly seemed possible.

We soon discovered that the Igreja Lusitana were interested in the idea, for two curious reasons. First, all their clergy, including the Bishop, had other full-time jobs, and so the idea of an ordained warden of a field study centre seemed quite natural. Secondly, they were not holding to a definitely traditional evangelical line that might have made them cautious about a Christian centre given over to environmental issues, although they were looking for help from BCMS which was clearly evangelical. Maybe like us they were pleasantly surprised by the changes that were taking place in evangelical thinking.

It was clearly time to talk again to Les. His wife Wendy had been as interested as Miranda by the idea, and was, indeed, similarly prepared to change her plans rapidly. So we spent a weekend together, and heard more of the way that they had envisaged a house open to all comers interested in natural history, but with a clear Christian character. They had been very impressed by the writings of the American philosopher and teacher Francis Schaeffer and what they had heard of the centre he had established in Switzerland called L'Abri. There, people with no particular religious commitment could be welcomed into a community to discuss and disagree. Hospitality played a big part in giving the community its distinctive character. There had been no particular environmental application although Francis Schaeffer had written a pioneering book, *Pollution and the Death of Man*, in 1970. Les had sketched out in a drawing the way the house might work. He saw the heart of the house as being family life, but with a series of environmental education projects reaching into the local community. They too had small children, Ruth and Hilary, but were obviously quite prepared to adapt their ideas and to consider working abroad. We could see that we were quite different as families, but as we talked and prayed we became aware that it was all becoming more substantial than just a good idea.

If we were going to take it any further we needed to go to Portugal to talk to people in conservation and the church. Here was the first problem: neither family had any money to pay for such a venture. We decided to put our convictions to the test and so we went ahead and booked the air tickets, agreeing to tell no one that we needed money to pay for them. We made an exception with the travel agents, out of fairness to them in case they were unwilling to sell us tickets in such unusual circumstances, but also because I think we were certain that the money would be there when it was needed. We thought it might be interesting for them to observe the process.

We had been trying ever since we began work in the parish to live our Christian experience "inside out", so that friends who were uncommitted could see what it was actually like, as opposed to hearing the official version in church. The experience had proved very worthwhile, if a little harrowing at times because life with a young family can be stressful, and the reality to an outsider looks very little like The Imitation of Christ. Nevertheless, despite all of that, some of our friends were becoming Christians, and so we were sufficiently bold to want to carry on the experiment. The baffled travel agents decided to take the risk and to humour us.

As the days passed, money began to arrive in extraordinary ways, one of the more memorable being the night when several houses in our road were broken into, while a hundred pounds in ten-pound notes lay in an envelope in our porch. We only discovered it in the morning. Late one afternoon, two months later, I returned from visiting the local hospital to hear that the travel agent had been on the phone to Miranda.

"Mrs Harris, you will probably realise that despite the unusual circumstances, these tickets must be paid for by the end of the afternoon."

"You'll have your money," she said.

By then we were still seven hundred pounds short, and her calm account of this conversation was highly alarming. I could well imagine that an embittered travel agent might have good reason for seriously espousing atheism faced with such irresponsible Christian behaviour. I also realised I had little clue of the penalties for obtaining air tickets under false pretences:

10

a week in Torremolinos perhaps? Was that why Benidorm was so crowded? Miranda's faith had been frightening, but the phone call from friends moments later to say that they had a thousand pounds to give us "for Portugal" was even more worrying. They knew nothing about our need to buy the tickets, but had recently become Christians and shortly afterwards had received a technical redundancy payment. They wanted it to be a gift of gratitude to God.

So we paid the travel agent, who was suitably intrigued. We seemed to be straying into the dangerous realm of the Christian paperback with the purple cover. I had never enjoyed books with titles like *Faith in the Fast Lane*, not least because we seemed to spend a fair amount of time on the hard shoulder.

How God makes his intentions clear to us seems to be a universal question among Christians, and particularly so among those about to make drastic changes in their lives. We found from the first that it was never easy to know what to do, and that clear-cut answers to basic questions can be hard to come by. However, after some years now of living rather near the edge at times, we have an absolute confidence in God's ability to guide us, and perhaps a reduced certainty of our willingness to be guided.

We were managed rather like babies in the early days of the project. It was as if we needed such unusually clear signals because things were at times so difficult that anything less than certainty about what was going on would have cast us adrift. We were treated to a startling sequence of coincidences rather like a private firework display, all the more interesting because it was unexpected. We were not aware that we would come to appreciate it so much later on when we needed every ounce of conviction to overcome the difficulties that arose. It has been said that coincidences happen to everyone, but they seem to happen more frequently to Christians. As we were more used to making our decisions in a rather commonsense fashion, working from general principles and leaning heavily on the advice of good friends and respected leaders, the show was fun while it lasted. Subsequently we have come to

11

understand that there is a distinction between God's promise to lead us and our awareness that he is doing so, which is rather a different thing.

We are currently living with a couple of provisional ideas which seem to fit quite well with what the Bible teaches, and which go a long way towards making sense of the loose ends we find after we think we've tied all the knots.

First, there is no blueprint for a perfect course of action which it is our job to identify. The idea that there is such a blueprint reduces the whole business to a kind of celestial game show with dire consequences for wrong guesses, but it seems to be widely believed. Presumably a wrong choice would invalidate the whole blueprint, but that is never explained.

Our second idea is that within a framework in which we are committed to obedience, God gives us real choices, and he works out his will within them from the infinite possibilities that are thereby raised. This is perhaps the Apostle Paul's meaning when he writes in Romans, chapter twelve that first of all our minds should be transformed, and then that we should be able to discern the perfect will of God. We grow up into godliness by creatively exercising the freedom God gives us to choose according to his will out of a desire to obey, rather than by recognising his will reluctantly and following it with a heavy sigh. These are genuine choices, and on occasions God leaves them to us to make. God does sometimes lead his people to specific things, as we were discovering, but at others there is no single correct answer to identify, and six wrong ones to eliminate.

Sometimes several possibilities will equally express the relationship of trust and obedience with God, and in wrestling with them the relationship grows. I have often enjoyed helping our youngest daughter Bethan to fill in the spaces between the dots in her writing exercises. As they get fewer she suddenly recognises the word she's writing, and what was mechanical suddenly gains meaning – great excitement! Great for learning to read and write, but a terrible way of thinking about the will of God. We are not required passively to follow a dotted line to heaven until suddenly the meaning of this mechanical process bursts on our inner eye. Rather God's meaning, what he intends, comes to us in the context of knowing him, much as a child gains knowledge of its grandparents, and learns that they love to read stories, but don't appreciate being hit by a water bomb from the top of the stairs. There are infinite possibilities for what they can do together, but it is shaped by the character of grandparents and children, and the relationship they have. Knowing who God is and loving him is the only way to finding out what he wants.

Paul again spells it out when writing to the Corinthians: "Knowledge puffs up, but love builds up. The man who thinks he knows something does not yet know as he ought to know. But the man who loves God is known by God."

The search to know the will of God may well begin with us wanting to find out more of the future, but it ends by our being drawn into relationship with the Father, and often thereby living comfortably with many uncertainties.

2

"Time spent in reconnaissance is seldom wasted." – sign above a Sandhurst dance-floor

All these ideas were being worked out as we began planning a reconnaissance trip to Portugal with Gordon Fyles of BCMS, using our precious tickets and the cheapest February package we could find.

We had decided early on that the Algarve seemed the most likely area. For centuries it had almost been forgotten, the old coins describing the rulers as "King of Portugal, and the Algarve", mentioning the province almost as an afterthought, a land apart in the south. Now it was visited by over a million people from all over Europe and beyond, and we hoped that this would enable us to give our centre an international character from the start. Furthermore, the volume of migratory bird traffic was even greater than the number of tourists. Strategically placed in the southwesternmost corner of continental Europe, the area was ideal for studies of migration. The mix of Atlantic and Mediterranean habitat types gave it a particular character, and there was work to do on nearly every aspect of its natural history.

When both families arrived in the Algarve in February 1983 there was very little to be seen of either international tourists or migrating birds. A cold wind blew through the mud-splashed alleys of the *urbanização* to which our package had brought us, and the abandoned orchards of figs nearby seemed

14

as empty of life as the streets. It was probably a good job that there were few ornithological distractions; we had just two weeks in which to meet as many people and to see as many places as we could, and then it would be time to decide if the project had a future.

The enquiries we had tried to make from England had not been very promising, not least because no one in the conservation world had answered any of our letters. As well as discovering whether the concept of the centre was right, we needed to find out whether we could settle the families in an area suitable for the project. So we began by investigating the schools.

The vagaries of the Portuguese school system at that time meant that there were often three- or four-hour gaps in the time-table. If we were going to live outside a town in a field study centre, this would pose real problems unless the children walked the streets all day. However, Les had heard of an international school which ran a bus service, so we went to investigate.

It was while we were talking to the head that we had our first really encouraging moment.

"Ah," she said, looking a little baffled as we explained what we were planning. "Yes, well we do have a couple on our staff who are religious like you."

As often happens when you talk openly about belief, we had the impression that she was half expecting us to break into plainsong at any moment.

"I'm sure they'll be fascinated to meet you," she continued uncertainly, probably thinking of the confusing array of Christian churches, and how the members of some of them might be less than fascinated to meet members of others. How difficult for an outsider to know which is which!

In the event, Tom and Edite Wilson were definitely as fascinated as we were and we met like lost relations, which I suppose in a way we were. For some years they had been ploughing a very lonely furrow in the Algarve, and they couldn't have been more welcoming. Tom was a Scot who had lived in Portugal for many years and had met and married

15

Edite when he was living in the north, and she was finishing her degree at Coimbra University. Edite was a considerable linguist having studied English and German, and was currently head of the Portuguese department of the school. Without hesitating she offered to be responsible for teaching us Portuguese.

It didn't end there. We agreed to meet after school so they brought their three children round, and as we all huddled round the fire in the rented villa we explained what we were hoping to do. They were immediately enthusiastic.

"Very few Protestants are involved outside the church in any area of society," Tom explained. "We have a ghetto mentality that goes back to the days of the dictatorship when there was genuine discrimination, and in some cases even persecution. That only ended with the Revolution in 1974 so it will take time to change. Even now there isn't complete religious tolerance, and the churches tend to approach society through a kind of raid-over-the-wall approach." He went on to tell us of one or two serious attempts that had been made at dialogue and explanation of the relevance of the gospel.

"You could have a real contribution to make, if only as a bridge-building exercise."

It seemed as though they were prepared to take our word for the importance of the environmental work.

After the bleak start we began to feel more cheerful. Tom and Edite took on some of the practicalities in a way which we later came to recognise as typical of their Scottish/Portuguese partnership. They would be happy to find us places to live if we told them the area. We could borrow their beloved and battered Renault 4 during the day while they were at school.

"What else might you need? Come round and talk about it at the weekend." The children's first contact with a family who didn't always speak English raised some questions for them. "Mum, Tom and Edite say grace to a Portuguese God they know," said Esther.

Even with Tom and Edite's enthusiastic endorsement, there were some difficult moments as we tried to translate our lofty vision into practical proposals. The weather was terrible, with

16

snow on the Serra de Monchique for the first time in forty years. We discovered why our package deal had been so cheap; no one was foolish enough to want a house in February that was plainly designed for the blazing days of July. Freezing rain came in through every part of the roof and lay in chilly puddles on the cold tile floors. Impressive colonies of ants were dug in for the winter in the brick bases of the beds, and took their daily exercise marching in columns across our pillows. The budget had stretched to renting only a baby Fiat, and we had echoes of forgotten jokes out of Christmas crackers ringing in our ears as we squeezed four adults and five children into the tiny seats. It is perhaps sufficient to point out that Jeremy was still in nappies to hint at the additional stresses of the situation, particularly in the frequent heavy rainstorms that rocked the car as we clattered up into the hills and down to the coast trying to imagine each old house as a possible future centre.

The prospect of living in an area so clearly headed for rapid and disastrous environmental change was not too exciting, so we weren't exactly elated. It was never going to be a rural idyll, and the Christian community was pitifully small. At least in Tanzania we could feel vaguely useful. "Well, I'll come if we are supposed to," said Miranda as we swung back into the town after another fruitless day peering through the rain at derelict cottages. "But it will have to be pretty clear, that's all." Beginning to feel that a clear-cut Bible teaching job some-where hot might have much to recommend it, all I could do was agree.

We had the long-suffering Fiat for three days only, and at the end of the second we could not say that we had seen anywhere that would really be suitable for what we were hoping to do. That evening we pored over the map for what felt like the twentieth time. We drew a twenty-kilometre circle around the school, and as we looked at the western edge we noticed for the first time the small estuary to the west of a village called Alvor.

From the moment we arrived by the shore of the estuary the next morning we could see that it might be all we had been looking for. The heavy rain clouds of the previous two days had moved off, the broad sandflats shimmered in the strong early morning sunlight, and the river was alive with waders and terns. Even the names of the beautifully painted boats hauled up on the mud seemed encouraging: *Deus o Nosso Esperança* (God Our Hope), and *Jesus me Guia* (Jesus Leads Me). In the land around the river we could see that there was a variety of habitats ranging from marshes to woodland, scrub and orchards. With one unfortunate exception where some tower blocks loomed over the back of the dunes, there had been little development to mar the beauty of the landscape. A pair of White Storks soared over the nearby farmland, and as we walked down to the edge of the water through an avenue of old carob trees carpeted with yellow oxalis we could finally imagine how it might be to share such a place with many others. The children rushed on ahead beneath the trees, and we all looked at each other: "This is it – this must be the place," said Miranda.

No one had mentioned the area to us, so it was probably little known, and certainly had no protected status; maybe we could contribute something by drawing attention to the area before it was engulfed by the tourist wave spreading west from Faro? If so we might not have very much time.

Later that evening Les and I went back with Tom in his redoubtable Renault 4. Tom's fluent Portuguese enabled us to locate the owner of much of the land surrounding the estuary. Apparently he rarely came down from Lisbon in the winter, but was here for just a few days. We decided to see how he would feel about having a field study centre for a neighbour. "This car will go anywhere," Tom cheerfully assured us in his broad Scots as we clattered down the rough track to the house by the shore. It was to become a kind of motto for some of the more hair-raising survey work we later had to do.

As we talked to Senhor Duarte, Tom's interpreting skills were a great help but not always essential. Even we could understand what he meant as he pointed to the small cannon he had mounted on his lawn overlooking the broad sandflats of the estuary.

"You see those tower blocks over there?" he said, his arm

waving towards the sprawling development on the far shore of the river.

"If they build another one I'm going to knock it down with this! Boom!"

He told us we could bring people on to his land for field studies "until eternity" but despite his hostility to the building on other people's land admitted that there were imminent plans to develop the estuary as a marina, and to build hotels and golf courses on his fields. There was no guarantee that the land would remain undeveloped for more than a few more months. It was our first encounter with the love-hate attitude to tourism which we later discovered to be widespread among people who both loved their land but had much to gain by selling it for building. In view of the difficulties of making a living any other way, it is easy enough to understand the problem.

Nevertheless, as we left him and headed back to our own tourist blackspot, we agreed that apart from the uncertainty hanging over the site, in every other way it was ideal. The centre we were planning would be used primarily by students, particularly from within Portugal, and there was a railway station within easy walking distance which would save a lot of transport problems. There were regular buses along the main road, a useful reassurance given that rail strikes were a feature of life at that time. Nearby were the two lively towns of Portimão and Lagos which both had very small protestant churches. The village of Vila Verde, no distance away across the almond orchards, had no protestant church for its two thousand or so inhabitants, so maybe in time we could start one? Either way, it would be a help to be able to get all our supplies from so close at hand.

Sr Duarte's large farm on the central peninsula reaching down between the two rivers of the estuary was called Quinta da Rocha and we decided to adopt the name A Rocha, the Rock, for the project because it seemed to do justice to all that we were planning – the beginning of field studies, geology, and the only sure foundation for the whole of life, the Rock who is Christ.

We were beginning to see that it all might be possible, and nearly everyone we spoke to was positive about the idea. I made a quick visit with Gordon to the north of the country to meet the Bishop and others from the Igreja Lusitana. By now, though, it was becoming a little difficult to assimilate all the information from so many different people. I had arranged to talk to a friend from university days who was now working with students in Lisbon, and the conversation at the airport became so absorbing that I completely forgot about the plane until well after it had left. I finally arrived back in the Algarve late and unpopular.

The obstacles seemed enormous, but there was more than enough to make us believe that the project had a future. So we returned to England after a fortnight of travelling around to begin preparing in earnest. When all the bills for the trip were paid, there was exactly one pound left in the account.

Once back in the UK we began to look for kindred spirits who might make up a support team. We had already discovered during the three years of the curacy that the church was exceptionally big-hearted, but as A Rocha began to take shape we saw its true character even more clearly. Without belonging to the church we could never have gone beyond the first stages with the idea. Friends began to pray for all the different things that the new project would need, and slowly they were assembled.

One of the church-wardens was Bob Pullan, a geography lecturer at Liverpool University. He had extensive experience of field work in the Mediterranean, and combined great faith with a professional understanding of the environment. When we began the process of setting up a charitable Trust, I went to ask him if he would consider leading a team of Trustees. After we had talked for a while he quietly said, "I'd be very happy to – my life is ready to take a new direction."

I remember thinking that this sounded a little drastic, but in retrospect it could be seen as something of an understatement. At the time none of us had any idea of the level of commitment that A Rocha was going to require of him and his family. We were far more cautious and realistic when we asked his successor, Alan Coverdale, to consider doing the same job, because we had seen how the Pullan household had been transformed at times into an A Rocha depot, and how Bob had been required to carry the weight of much of the uncertainty that accompanied the early years. At times Alan has also found that A Rocha has threatened to fill his waking thoughts leaving little room for anything else.

We were greatly helped also by the august group who agreed to join our Council, because from the first we faced questions about the seriousness of any "mission work" that was concerned with the environment and the protection of wildlife. John Stott has a worldwide ministry as a theologian and writer, but also has an almost legendary passion for ornithology. Perhaps it betrayed him into giving credence to such an off-beat project, but he has been the leading advocate of a return to social involvement by evangelicals, and so he was immediately supportive of what we were proposing. Martin Goldsmith, a lecturer at All Nations Christian College, had been in the forefront of stirring up the British church to consider the claims of world mission, and was keen for any new initiatives. Professor Rowland Moss was lecturing in human ecology, but was one of the very few to be writing and talking from a biblical standpoint about the urgent need to address ecological problems. Each one has remained closely in touch with events at A Rocha, and they have subsequently been joined by Sam Berry, Professor of Genetics at London University, who has brought a Christian perspective to his involvement in a wide range of environmental issues.

At a local level there was practical help from literally hundreds of people. Some pounded out letters, others designed leaflets or hosted meetings. We were told of Trusts who might support us, and several times a day the phone rang with suggestions of possible supporters, or people who would be interested in A Rocha. We began to discover that there were a considerable number of Christians working in conservation, but that for many of them, their faith and their professional life were in hermetically sealed compartments. Some were intrigued by a project that hoped to bring the two together.

Nigel Walker, our long-suffering vicar, reconciled himself to the fact that his curate was going to spend half his final months establishing the support for a bird observatory in Portugal. Even so, there were some good moments in Upton as Nick and Alison Nichols, who were printing the literature, and Bernie and Jan Gallivan, who were making A Rocha sweatshirts, began to get more involved in the church, and then became Christians. A friend who was the warden of a local bird reserve joined their Bible studies, and soon had several people going out birding, while in turn they explained what being a Christian meant. Les and Wendy meanwhile had been finding that their friends were equally interested in the new project, and they were able to call on the network of people who had been following Les's earlier plans for a centre in England. They were heady days, and within six months there was a mailing list of four hundred supporters throughout the UK and beyond. Without their commitment and interest none of what followed would have been possible.

A letter arrived from Tom and Edite to say that they had been able to find rented accommodation for both families in a seaside town not far from where they lived, Armação de Pêra. There were places for the children at the school; were we going to come? The decision rested with the team of Trustees which was now complete: Bob and David Mann had environmental expertise, David Ager would take care of the legal side of the Trust, and Alan Ritchie the finances; Gordon Fyles would act as our contact with BCMS. When they met for the first time in July there were sufficient funds to see us through the first year, so the decision was taken to go ahead.

When it came to it, leaving Upton was a kind of bereavement. A short time on the staff of a church is enough to get to know people very well, not least because often you accompany them through some of their worst and best moments. Few things affect people so deeply as belonging to a church, if they will do it wholeheartedly, and St Mary's was a very wholehearted church. We had been with friends as they went through serious illnesses and nervous breakdowns, as their marriages had failed or hung by a thread. With others we had watched as

23

they had met and married, or had been thought unable to have children and then had them, or been made redundant and then found work again. Even the place meant a lot to us. Ever since the street party to celebrate the royal wedding, nearly everyone in the road had been much more open and friendly, and a strong sense of community had grown up. Quite a few had become Christians during the time we lived there, and we had really enjoyed being part of something which was quite unusual in our experience. During any day there were a hundred casual moments in which our identity in the heart of this community was affirmed. Now all of that was being put on one side in favour of something that didn't yet exist. There were times when we really wondered if we were mad, and we had a few letters that suggested we were leaving a going concern for a non-starter, and that to leave England was a kind of dereliction of duty.

So, despite a wonderful send-off, we arrived at Faro airport at the end of September 1983 with rather mixed feelings. As we stepped off the plane, the early evening was heavy with dust, and fragrant with the scent of pines and eucalyptus. It was oppressively hot and the humidity was so great that the air felt as though it was wrapping itself around us. We went

through the passport check to a baleful appraisal from the officer on the desk (local bureaucracy often isn't particularly user-friendly until you can chat for a while), and waited for our cases while the children clattered around on the luggage trolleys in the echoing hall. Then, as always when we moved house during the ensuing months, they took it all in their stride. Home was where we were, and that was it. Their unquestioning security was often a consolation to Miranda and me when we were feeling anything but settled anywhere. After all we should have known already what Jesus had spelt out. Home is with the Father, and has little to do with where you live, or even who you live with. Learning to feel that, as well as to know it, was one of the big lessons of the first couple of years in Portugal.

Tom was there to meet us as he had promised, ferrying us to spend the first night in their home before going over to our rented places in Armação de Pêra the next morning. The Portuguese end of A Rocha had finally begun. There were the five of us plus a student friend, Les and Wendy with Ruth and Hilary, and a total of some twelve suitcases between us. Had that been the only baggage, life would have been a lot more straightforward; but of course it soon became apparent that we were all carrying expectations and assumptions that we hadn't had time to unpack together in the heady days as first plans were made, and soon this led us to much mutual heart-ache and many doubts.

3

"Old donkeys don't learn Latin." – Portuguese proverb

Our first day began with a great sense of promise. We stood on the flat *terraço* of Tom and Edite's house as the sun came up and looked out towards the *serra* inland. This might be Europe, but with the landscape burnt to differing shades of brown after the heat of the summer, it looked and smelt more like Africa. Perhaps one day we might feel at home here. Either way it was going to be an adventure (although fairness compels me to say that over the years the children have come to recognise the phrase as synonymous with their parents making the best of some disaster or other).

The postal address of the house we were going to rent translated very promisingly as Palm Tree Alley number two, but we were a little dismayed to discover that it was embedded among night clubs and bars. Even so, the proximity of the beach made up for a lot, and the children were more than happy to have heavy metal music until four in the morning if it meant you could live next to a place that sold ice-creams until midnight. There hadn't been a lot of home-made pistachio ice-cream at any time of the day in Oakland Drive, Upton.

We unpacked, and then went over to inspect Les and Wendy's flat. It seemed fine except for the fact that there was no water. "Tomorrow," their landlord said cheerfully, and had not Tom been there looking faintly amused, I'm ashamed to say our cultural adaptation had progressed so little that we would have believed him. The word *amanhã* didn't sound sufficiently like *mañana*. We understand now that it doesn't carry the same sense of urgency either. However, it all served to emphasise that the first task was to learn all we could about the country, and of course to learn to speak Portuguese.

We now think it is a beautiful language, but at first we could not agree whether it sounded more like Spanish with a plum in your mouth or Russian spoken through the ears. We had baffling encounters with Maria Alice who came at the behest of the landlord to clean the little house we were renting. Was this a message about bread or about tomorrow? Her husband did what to her? Who was he, the torturer in the local jail or something? One day she arrived with a black eye and so we realised at least some of what we'd understood wasn't far wrong, but even so it was very hard for us all to live with such incomprehension.

I still wonder about the first person we talked to about the gospel and who apparently accepted it all. What kind of heretic did he become? I'm sure his view of the Godhead isn't restricted to the three persons of the Trinity but probably includes several vegetables and some items of furniture which we had desperately dredged up from our minuscule vocabulary in our struggle to communicate. Someone has said that the experience of going to live in another culture and language is like returning to childhood, and it certainly seemed so to us. We were helpless and dependent, clumsy and foolish.

More than that, we soon discovered that learning another language together was a psychological minefield. As we have subsequently heard others explain, it touches all too easily on our fear of being inadequate and resurrects ungodly responses to failure and competition, many of which date back to schooldays. As usual we broke all the rules through ignorance, and learned Portuguese in a group of four, which inhibited and frustrated us all. Apparently you should never learn a language with someone whose opinion you value, because it makes you far too vulnerable, and because everyone learns differently. We know that now, and have the scars to prove it. Nevertheless, as Miranda's journal recorded, the lessons were a help: "We

27

went over to Les and Wendy's flat for a conversation lesson and learnt a lot of useful phrases such as '*Não atire contre mim, estou a estudar pássaros; não quero incomodar nem fazer mal. O cão não morde?*' Which roughly translated means 'Please don't shoot me, I'm only studying birds and don't want to disturb you or do any harm. Does your dog bite?'"

The Mediterranean climate is much misunderstood in the north of Europe. Given the weight of the huge publicity machine that serves the package holiday business this is not surprising. That year there had been posters all over London that rather ingenuously showed a beach somewhere in the Caribbean above the legend "Winter isn't winter in Portugal". In the depths of the British winter we had been prepared to give them the benefit of the doubt, but we were therefore totally unprepared when the heavens opened in mid-October, and the autumn rains began in earnest. I received my first clue of what was to come during a bird survey when I optimistically took shelter under a tree in time-honoured English fashion, only to find that Portuguese rain has no respect for such flimsy obstacles. The phrase "soaked to the skin" does no justice to the almost intestinal state of damp to which I was reduced, and I returned home to find that Miranda's moment of enlightenment had come when she took her shoes out of the cupboard to find that overnight they had turned green with mould. The bathroom walls would have made an excellent field trip for lichenologists as they turned from rose pink to grey to black. We had no heating and so damp clothes were draped over every available surface – to the delight of Esther and Jeremy who made tents and nomad encampments in every room.

It rained solidly for a month, and only the remarkable passage of Leach's Petrels offshore in the break between storms was a consolation. (I'm reconciled to the fact that not all my readers may have had their eyes opened to the delights of watching seabirds in a force eight gale and driving rain, and so must explain that Leach's Petrel is a small, mostly dark seabird, a nocturnal visitor to land except when driven close inshore by foul weather. In the Algarve they are seen only once every few years.) Our neighbours, many already apparently in mourning, adopted an even more funereal appearance as they shuffled from doorway to doorway shrouded in black cardigans and huddled under raven-like umbrellas. Why, we wondered, did no one own a raincoat? We soon discovered when we tried to use ours and found that they were as effective as swimming costumes against the torrents of rain. The counterpoint to these trials was a steady stream of envious letters from friends in England. In their imagination we sprawled on the beach after a pleasant day observing the feeding habits of the common robin, and the sun set in a gentle glow behind our pioneering heads. We began to be aware that we had launched a public relations disaster.

Our friends from the south of England had murmured sympathetically as we moved to a curacy in Upton because the postal address was Merseyside. The move was invested with a noble air, hinting as it did at urban deprivation. On moving to Portugal, even worse the Algarve, and worse still to work for nature conservation, we became a lost cause. The Christian world is no more immune to the impact of fashion and image than any other.

We soon realised there was little to be gained by explaining that we felt much more isolated, and were physically less comfortable, than we had ever been in England. We had lost a lot of points on the heroism scale, and there was nothing to be done about it. Furthermore there was going to be little to show for A Rocha for some time to come. The centre didn't exist, and neither did anything like it anywhere else which could point to what we would be doing. No one knew if conservation would be a valid and practical expression of the concerns of world mission. While we were persuaded it would be, there was at times a sense of unreality. We were not the only ones to be surprised by the photo of a Honey Buzzard on the front cover of a mission magazine that reported the beginnings of A Rocha. One or two newspapers had taken a wry interest, and we had a small collection of bizarre news-paper cuttings like the one from the *Guardian*: "Curate Seeks Calling in Bird Haven". To several reporters the Lusitanian Church was the icing on the cake, sounding as it did like something out of a Gilbert and Sullivan opera, and the Vic-torian ring of the Bible Churchman's Missionary Society was the perfect adjunct to round off the story.

As a working life, it was certainly different. Instead of visiting, speaking, preaching and leading meetings we were, for the time being at least, inarticulate and unable even to understand our neighbours let alone to help them. Far from being at the hub of a busy church, even the small and scattered congre-gations in our area would not welcome any help, because we didn't belong to their denominations. Once school hours were over and Tom had his car back, we had no transport, and the buses to fetch the car were irregular. Frequently we would spend an hour or more by the side of the road waiting for one to turn up. This was a far cry from the high-speed, highly mobile life of a curate with four wheels and five hospitals to visit before teatime. (Not that I am recommending it; all too easily it can become two wheels and then a sixth hospital.)

It wasn't easy to study Portuguese with two children under three sharing the same room, and so we copied the local students and took turns to sit in the café making the powerful black coffee stretch for an hour at a time with our books spread over the table. The strong dose of caffeine produced a fifteen-minute surge of fluency, followed by forty-five minutes of growing despair as the crashing metabolism battled with verbs which veered off in ever more unpredictable directions. All the essential verbs had started off as Latin, which was bad enough, but had then become gnarled and worn by constant use. The little orchard of these verbs cost more to acquire than the vast serried plantation of others that we might need once every couple of years if, for example, we had to get binoculars mended, or to thread a fishing hook. Portuguese thinking is deeply embedded in the language, and so it was not simply a question of learning what it might be correct to say, but how in fact you would say it. A simple phrase like "When you come on Wednesday" reveals all kinds of suppositions. In English we contemplate a certain future (most unwisely in this part of the world at least), and so much of the time we don't even bother with a future tense. In Portuguese the future is very much an unknown quantity, and so the verbs shy away into subjunctives to give due consideration to all that unpre-dictability – "Should you come on Wednesday . . ." Further-more, any promise to meet on a future occasion was followed by "*Se Deus quiser*" – Should God will it – not so much out of any deep belief in God as profound suspicion that it might not happen. Not only did we need to think Portuguese before we could truly be said to speak it, but we needed to understand the beliefs woven into what was said. We were surprised to discover that there was much that was Islamic in character although the five centuries of Moorish occupation had ended nearly eight hundred years ago.

It was not only in Portuguese that we were complete begin-ners. Until we had spent some time on the first field studies, we had little to contribute to conservation. There seemed to be everything to learn and nothing to pass on, and it made us aware that we were not well equipped to understand the experience. It was difficult to understand what it could mean to serve God if we were not being useful, and it revealed a series of little sub-heresies which were lodged in our thinking. As some of our friends responded to our first reports of what

31

we were doing in the Algarve we realised that we weren't alone in our confusion.

Sub-heresies is a reasonable description for these wayward ideas because they are rarely articulated, but nevertheless they form a powerful part of the package of assumptions held by many churches. We had often assumed that the most important thing about the Christian life was its usefulness to God and to others. For example, on Wednesday mornings in the parish I had five school assemblies or services in different places before eleven a.m. Consequently it was very easy to value what we did simply because we were very busy doing it, and very tired once it was done! By contrast now we had finally arrived in Portugal, we seemed to spend hours in offices simply trying to overcome the bureaucratic obstacles to living here, without being able to get on with what we had come to live here for. The regulations were frequently wonderfully circular, and we survived by savouring each new problem like connoisseurs. The local office of the foreigners' department carried on the user-friendly tradition with which we were now familiar. It was tucked away at the most obscure end of a distant corridor on the top floor of the nineteenth-century council building. The twists and turns involved in navigating your way to the door would have tested the skills of the first Portuguese

explorers. Once at the door there was a bench, and the meaning of the bench was all too clear. This is a place where you wait. I learned more irregular verbs sitting on that bench than at any bus-stop, the other sticking point in the daily routine. Once we finally gained access to the mysteries behind the door, the message was as follows: If you want to apply for a residence permit, you must be living outside the country, but in practice you cannot complete the process without living in the country, which you cannot do without a residence permit. And so on. We tried to see it as good language practice, particularly in the use of the negative prefix to verbs, and the correct pronunciation of the adjective *impossível*.

We had an early letter from John Ball that warned us that initially we would feel of very little use in Portugal, and he made it clear that no one was looking for any results for some time to come. Even so, we still found it hard to shake off the habits of mind that we had adopted in England while we had been doing a completely different job. In common with many others we knew we placed a high value on being immediately effective. This probably originated from the priorities established by business and commerce, but it had become accepted widely in the church. The important questions were put in terms such as: does the Kingdom of God benefit numerically or in any other quantifiable way by what we are busy with? Can the results of our activity be evaluated easily? How time-efficient are our lives?

The problem with seeing our work for A Rocha in terms like that wasn't simply that so much of our time seemed wasted at bus-stops and in offices. It had more to do with the work of A Rocha as a conservation project. We had been drawn to the idea of A Rocha because by insisting on the importance of creation to the church the project seemed to challenge some of these little deviations from biblical truth. Now it came to it, we found we were too fragile to enjoy the early explanations and battles with Christian convention. From day to day we had to live with far less affirmation than we had been used to in the UK. We were essentially on our own with the problems, and therefore we undoubtedly became over-sensitive to any suggestion of criticism. We know now that this is a common experience for people working outside their own culture, but at the time we didn't realise it.

Nevertheless we had no alternative but to persevere, and not merely because we were trying to establish nature conservation as a necessary concern for the church. Although the issue was thrown into relief by the work we were doing, principally because nature conservation and field studies can seem irrelevant to human problems, we began to see that the problem went wider than that. There are large areas of human experience that cannot be seen as productive or efficient. It is not necessary to be working in nature conservation to discover how many and varied they are.

An obvious example is any form of artistic activity, and it is notable that only recently has evangelical thinking broadened sufficiently to value the work done by artists of various kinds. Even now there is a suspicion that art is more worthwhile if it serves some evangelistic end. Other less exalted occupations that would have to be rated as spiritually sterile include simple tasks like changing nappies or washing up, or even making a living. They are hard to defend if we look for them to be effective for the kingdom of God, and might therefore be seen as time wasted. The sooner they are done and we can get back to more productive pursuits the better, we may feel.

There is no biblical foundation for such a reduced view of human life. It is challenged from the first chapter of Genesis through to many of the Psalms, particularly Psalm 84 and Psalm 63. Matthew 22: 34–40 and Romans 12: 1–2 go on to make it clear that if we must categorise human activity, then none is more important for a human being than worship, an inefficient and unproductive activity if ever there was one. Quite apart from the general drift of the biographies of many of the characters in scripture, it is challenged by the periods of apparent inactivity that are imposed by God on many of them. Supremely it is thrown into question by the life of Jesus himself as he awaits the right moment for his public ministry and then can be seen to withdraw at times once it has begun, apparently in the interests of who he is, and his relationship with the Father, rather than to maximise the efficiency of what he does.

Finally, if we are honest about the everyday realities of our lives, about how we actually spend our time, we cannot believe that God could only be interested in the limited period which we can describe as useful. In a lifetime, there is simply too little of it! While we were working for a church it might have been possible to identify clearly which parts of our lives were of greater interest and importance to God, and which were irrelevant to him. Now we were working for A Rocha it became impossible. Necessarily all the parts of our life belonged to the whole which was given over to this particular project. The struggle was to understand where all we were doing, productive or not, fitted in and took its place in the over-arching context of life in Christ. We were not seeking merely to understand the apparently religious elements of our human experience, but all of it. We had been led towards the work of A Rocha because our deeply felt response to the natural world became gradually more insistent. Intuitively a deep-ening relationship with God seemed to make all we saw in the world around us more vivid, more striking and more beautiful. More consciously, understanding the value that God himself gave to his world meant it was harder to stand by and do nothing about the growing number of ways in which the world was being damaged. Even the limited awareness that we had of the world around was constantly affirmed by our relation-ship with God and by scripture. We have spoken since to many others who have taken up the same search, and are trying to make sense of the same strong response to creation, or to art in different forms. We have also encountered quite a few who have given up the unequal struggle and settled for a compart-mentalised spirituality which brings to mind the abandoned farmlands of the Algarve. If you stand on any hill and look around you, it is a fragmented landscape. There are small fruitful areas of cultivated fields, but they are set among wide areas of untended and barren land, the scrub enveloping the old orchards of figs, almonds and carob, a silent witness to a losing battle.

From our very first days in rented accommodation, visitors from the UK began to appear at the door holding leaflets about A Rocha which they had been given by friends, or articles about the project from magazines. Some were interested in A Rocha because they had found no other Christians in the area; others because they wanted to know where to go birding, or where to find orchids, or because they needed help of some kind. We spent some time in the field together if possible, and there were often opportunities to talk about some of the things we were discovering.

As we spent time with different people observing what happens in the natural world, it confirmed our growing convictions. There were constant reminders that we could not explain everything we saw purely in terms of its function. Much of the beauty of a Woodlark's song, or the colours of a Bee-eater's plumage, goes well beyond what might be seen as necessary for the bird's biological effectiveness, and speaks of the artistic activity of a creator working to a different set of priorities than what is merely useful or efficient. As we talked with those of our visitors who were Christians about what we were watching, we frequently heard the same lament. Often they battled with a burden of guilt because they had been unable to reconcile much that they instinctively valued, or were drawn by their personalities or natural gifts to do, with the inadequate priorities of a system that seemed to place effectiveness above any other virtue.

So we began to explain the background to our own struggle, much of which owed itself – as did that of many of our visitors – to the conviction that our feeling for the natural world was in fact God-given, and made sense in ways for which we could construct no explanation, given the toolkit of teaching which we had at the time. One missing spanner from the toolkit was teaching about creation. It was a common cause of the difficulty that we and others had found in making sense of that side of our lives. The usual emphasis of much Christian teaching frequently neglected a vital element in the Old Testament, in effect almost a modern-day flowering of the Marcionite heresy of the second century, which rejected the Old Testament. The

New Testament writers understood well from their scriptures, the Old Testament, that the creation was important, and that the whole of life had an intimate setting in the character of God. It was the background for all their thinking. Although such ideas do not form a natural part of our understanding when we read the New Testament today, once they are neglected we are in danger of seeing only one side of the biblical coin. In reality the coin has two sides, and with care both can be found in both Testaments: there is teaching about creation and teaching about redemption. The former has to do with the world and all of human experience, the latter to do with the church and the new creation, including our invitation to the Kingdom of God.

As we continued to give time to the different bird studies, and reflected on what we were doing with others, a great many strands began to come together, and the resulting rope of ideas exerted a strong pull. Maybe by giving new thought to how important the creation was to God we could help others to discover and value a neglected part of themselves which was part of their created humanity? Maybe as we encouraged others to give time to careful observation and study, something of the character of God would be revealed, because the world is his handiwork and speaks of his nature? We would be handling the raw material of redemption, building a stage on which the drama of salvation could be acted out. We would be pursuing Christian mission, but through creation and not simply through the more familiar side of the coin which involves witnessing to redemption alone.

Perhaps it was the lack of a creation perspective in Christian thinking and activity that went some way towards explaining the sense of unease that some of our visitors felt about the church. Both committed Christians and others sometimes expressed dismay that the churches they knew seemed to take so little account of primary, human, created things. They saw the church as preoccupied with the church, and so concluded that its activities must be of interest principally to church people, defined as people interested in religion, much as others were interested in fishing or volleyball.

Those who were not believers were left with the impression that Christianity had little to do with the desperate state of the world around. Those who were Christians, but who were drawn by temperament or by their gifts towards an interest in creation, usually found that there were few possibilities for involvement and service among the available options.

In these discussions, we could only agree that while Christians believe the truth of "Christ in us, the hope of glory", and in the power of the Holy Spirit to transform our instincts and our behaviour, it is sadly true that we often apply a careful veto to the expression of that new life, maybe out of an exaggerated fear of the remaining faults and follies of our unrenewed nature. Although we live in an in-between age where the Kingdom of God has yet to be completely consummated, we could give more credit to the creativity and spontaneity of the new life of the Kingdom of God that has already been brought into the world.

There is no doubt that some found the lamentable state of their local church a useful excuse for avoiding a serious encounter with the gospel, but it was undeniable that the casual contacts with the church described by the majority of our uncommitted visitors had only been a hindrance to their understanding of God. It may well be that this was because those churches had ceased to understand him as Creator.

In recent years there has been a considerable change, and we were able to talk about churches we knew which affirmed their members, and equipped them for involvement in society. It was more difficult to cite instances of churches which had a serious interest in the created world to the point of altering their communal lifestyle in obedience to God-given convictions.

By no means everyone we talked to about these things during A Rocha's early months understood what we meant, but others recognised what we were trying to do and saw parallels with their own struggles. Sometimes it was very humbling. The church of St John's Chrysostom in Everton is arguably set in one of the most depressing environments of any city, and yet they decided to support A Rocha as part of their commitment to BCMS. They told us that they were working for the same goals despite the completely different surroundings. Maybe because they too have needed to develop a completely new approach to church life in order to survive in the highly unstable and irregular world of the housing estates in the area, they have been among our most understanding supporters from the beginning. For ourselves, we have always been aware that we could easily develop an escapist approach, tucked away in what Algarveans fondly call *o nosso cantinho*, our little corner. We were grateful for churches like St John's which allowed us to check what we were doing against the daily experience of Christians in very different contexts. Not that our daily experience was always too far removed from that on Merseyside. The interminable process of being assessed for Family Income Supplement at our local office in Birkenhead was very good preparation for the more picturesque corridors of Portimão.

4

"We don't know the ins and outs, how should we? how could we?"
– David Jones

One morning in November, having done our time on the
bench and finally gained admission to the Foreigners' Service
holy of holies, we were able to understand enough of the
fierce discussion that was raging to realise why our papers
continued to be so delayed.

I cannot deny that the Portuguese way of doing things seems
inexplicably inefficient to the British (as it does to many Portuguese), but the Portuguese for their part are quite reasonably
convinced that the British are terminally bonkers. They have
been unable to find any other explanation for our bizarre
behaviour over the last couple of centuries. Having observed
with polite curiosity the highly eccentric preoccupations of
early visitors to the north of the country, they now watch with
horrified fascination the startling spectacle of a million or so
tourists in the south inflicting severe epidermal damage on
their alabaster-pale bodies by lying out in the full midday sun
each summer.

So it was not surprising that we merely reinforced the
stereotype when we appeared in the Foreigners' Service with
a piece of paper from a Portuguese bishop (church unknown,
but something to do with Terry Waite, the only Anglican of
whom they had ever heard) purporting to explain that the
undersigned bishop hoped we would spend our time studying

birds on his behalf. The meaning of the knowing looks across the office desks was all too clear: more British *maloucos*. Even so, despite the raised voices, it seemed as though everyone in the office had been drawn into the debate, and the issue was being examined at an impressively high level. The argument ranged from the proper concerns of Christian belief and specifically about its relevance to the eco-crisis, to the origins of the Episcopate. The well-known lunatic tendencies of the English race within the British population were summarised in a comprehensive historical review. Eventually, despite a powerful plea from a lady who kept rabbits and who therefore apparently felt an affinity with us for reasons that our limited command of Portuguese failed to reveal, we were refused permission to stay in Portugal. We left the office highly alarmed and saw an ignominious end to all we had hoped to do.

"No problem at all," Tom and Edite patiently explained as we reappeared looking crestfallen on their doorstep that evening. "It's just a step in the dance."

Once again they took over and started to do things the right way, beginning with a phone call to a relative who was high up in the ministry. Cultural lesson number fifty-six completed, we breathed again. Meanwhile we continued to live out of the suitcases until such time as we could import any of our belongings.

41

The first real sign of permanence in Portugal came with the arrival of the Red Rose Our Valentine, a second-hand Renault 4, purchased on February 14th and named by Esther in a suffusion of joy as we careered round the empty streets of Armação that night. The children had supposedly been sleeping, but they heard the car when I pulled up outside, and piled out into the street in their night things, so off we all went on a celebratory ride. She was all the more special for being the gift of the church in Cranham where Miranda's sister Anita, and her husband Charlie Cleverly who was the curate, were working. It is a church full of faith which probably explains how the Red Rose survived so long on the lethal roads of the Algarve. She remained the A Rocha workhorse for many years until she finally came to an ignominious end, run down at the junction outside Portimão by a hired car full of tourists. (Although they drove off at high speed, they were overhauled in a Los Angeles-style manoeuvre by a council official whose sympathies lay firmly on the side of what he correctly deduced from the dust was a local car. They got her only just before the rust did but we all grieved her passing, and the arrival of her successor, a white Renault 4 van promptly named The Fridge – financed with far less faith and certainly no prayer by the Red Rose's long-suffering insurance company – was a muted affair by comparison.)

Once freed from the need to borrow Tom's car whenever we wanted to get off the bus routes, we resumed the trips to the different areas where we had begun some modest field work.

I started a regular count of the birds that were found around the Alvor estuary. In many bird counts, it is more important to note down the different calls than to try to see everything because your ears can operate in all directions simultaneously. More than that, I soon discovered that on the hotter days many of the local warblers seemed to spend their time deep in the aromatic bushes and shrubs, and were hard to observe. While I knew how to identify the birds if they ever allowed themselves to be seen, it took time to build up the basic vocabulary of calls. The books weren't a lot of help since about sixty species seemed to make "a distinctive short 'tchut'". Walking around the area also gave me frequent opportunities to try out the other vocabulary which I had to master, because it was impossible to get very far in the countryside without alarming someone's dogs. I usually found that the grammatical niceties of our hard-won phrases were abandoned in the heat of the moment, but then long explanations in the yard by the cottage would follow.

"You are watching birds? Of course there's none left now. What the hunters don't shoot, the ants get in the nest. Now if you had come thirty years ago, the orchards were full of them." Soon afterwards the conversation would go down familiar lines which were less testing on my limited language skills. "Are you looking for a house to buy? As it happens, this one is for sale." Everyone was trying to sell their place if they owned it, and sometimes if they didn't. It seemed as though in the Algarve, all conversational roads led to money. Finally I would try to make my excuses and leave, explaining that I had to get back to my work. "You are working here? What do you do? You do *this*? You mean someone is *paying* you to count birds?"

Although it was hardly the whole story, I could scarcely believe it either, and it was obvious that I would need to be far more fluent before I would ever be able to explain.

We knew very little about the environment of the Algarve, and it appeared that little had been published, so basic surveys were in order. We had decided early on to make bird studies our first aim, partly because they were what interested us most, but also because it was a form of natural history easily accessible to visitors to an eventual centre. Birds are good indicators of the health of any natural environment, living as they do at a furious metabolic rate, and also occupying a vulnerable position at the top of the ecosystem.

Les had been visiting the inland areas, and through his work we began to be familiar with which birds were found in the different habitats, and to discover which habitats were rare and which widespread. We also began to understand some of the forces at work in the landscape which were causing it to change so fast. Chief among them of course was tourism. As we drove each day along the Algarve's main road, soon to be classified the second most dangerous in Europe following the infamous marginal near Lisbon, we could see new buildings and roads at every turn. Many business signs were in English, and every mile we passed builders' yards and billboards, furniture shops and restaurants. The transformation was as radical as any imposed by a colonial power on a subject nation, and obeyed far fewer controls.

There has always been a considerable irony in the fact that it is people from the more environmentally aware countries of the north of Europe who have caused such destruction in the south. By the time they arrive at their holiday destination, the damage is already done and the original pinewoods, or marsh, or rare coastal maquis, have all been cleared and it is impossible to imagine the loss. Inevitably the visitors have little commitment to the environment of a place where they stay so briefly, and then only for its climate and not for anything characteristic of the area. Everyone is passing through, so no one feels he belongs in the area or has any concern for its well-being. Those who come to live there in order to develop it for tourism are usually concerned only to make a profit. Many coastal areas in the Mediterranean have never been more than sparsely occupied, and by people with little access to decision-making or power. They too have often exhausted the landscape in the harsh struggle to make a living on marginally fertile land. The combination of fire, overgrazing by goats and sheep, destruction of the woodlands and overfishing has left little future for many areas apart from the tourist bonanza.

Against the background of the transient population of tourists, and distant conservation decrees, we were going to have to put down some roots if we were to be of any use to the community and its environment. It was the only way to understand how the natural world of the Algarve worked, and to help to provide accurate information to assess the changes that were taking place, so that something could be salvaged before it was too late.

However, before we could start to build foundations any-

where in a community, we had a problem to resolve. As our first winter in Portugal came to an end, it became increasingly obvious that the two families had different ideas about which area would be the best one to go for. Les had worked for some years at the Medina Valley Centre in the Isle of Wight, and was ready for a change from estuarine habitats. He was drawn to the inland hills and valleys, while I had remained with our original conviction that the Alvor estuary would be an ideal site.

The only solution was to move from Armação de Pêra where both families were still living, and to explore different areas before coming to a decision about where the centre should be. Les and Wendy went inland to Silves, a traditional community under the walls of the old Moorish castle at the foot of the hills leading up to the Serra de Monchique. We decided to move west to the village of Vila Verde which was within walking distance of the Alvor estuary.

Once again we enlisted Tom Wilson's help and unfailingly cheerful company as we began the search for a flat. He had a well-developed technique for inspecting the different places that we considered renting. "I'd just like to have a wee look at the outside," he'd mutter, although we were puzzled by the interest that the identical whitewashed walls could have for tenants, particularly ones who were going to live on the second floor. It soon transpired that he knew that the prospective landlord would always offer us, in terms that could not decently be refused, some of the lethal local brandy, made from the fruit of the *medronheira*, the strawberry tree which grows on the *serra*. In order to minimise the risk of incurring brain damage, it is usually reckoned to be advisable to know the person who has brewed the stuff; as we didn't, Tom was simply marking out the best place to deposit the contents of his glass. Failing a garden, any flower pot would do, and our tour around the various flats to rent in the village could probably have been charted some hours later by the trail of dying plants, fatally dosed with *medronho*. In the end, after several false starts and one or two no-hopers including a kind of scout-hut at the top of the village (it was the Brussels sprouts

46

that caught it on that occasion, I remember), we finally found a good little flat above Isabel's hairdressing salon. We subsequently discovered that she had neglected to tell Oscar her husband that she was renting the flat which was their home, and that they were moving in downstairs with her parents and the hairdryers, but more of that later.

The flat was small, but a great improvement on the dark and damp little house in Armacao. On the first morning we woke to the scent of the orange trees, and the sun pouring through the windows, and knew that we would love the place. Oscar and Isabel had called in a mason to remove a stone shelf so that we could put a cooker into the kitchen, and he arrived just as we were finishing breakfast. "Don't worry about moving anything," he said, "I'll only be a moment." Such was our ignorance of the optimism that we now know attends all such jobs in Portugal, that we decided to leave him to it and go out for a walk. As we rounded the corner a hundred yards from the house on our way back an hour later, we could hear his power saw still tearing into the stone. The kitchen lay under an even layer of white dust several inches thick, and in the middle a ghostly figure was studying the seven-inch cut in the slab. "Have to get a new blade before the next one," he remarked confidently. "Not long now." By late afternoon he had left, and we began the clearing up.

Fortunately, no other major alterations were necessary, and the flat even boasted a fireplace, which was all Miranda normally needs to feel at home anywhere. However, we weren't sure we could live with the series of multicoloured glass spheres that cascaded down to light the table; they tended to give a fevered carnival atmosphere to the simplest breakfast, so we stored them on top of the wardrobe in our tiny room, and weathered Isabel's reproachful glances. The alterations to the amazing chandelier in our room were less intentional. The whole edifice was hung with porcelain roses, suspended on bits of wire. I was always forgetting that they hung within range, and fired them into different corners of the room every time I took off my shirt. Fortunately we found most of them by the time it came to leave.

47

Over the following months, we went over every week in the Red Rose to spend time with Les and Wendy in Silves. As we talked and prayed together, it was clear to us all that our ideas about how the project should go forward were diverging even further. It became increasingly difficult for the Trustees to reconcile the different directions being suggested to them, and in visiting us Bob Pullan had to discover diplomatic gifts he never knew he had. Eventually Les and Wendy felt that what they wanted to do could no longer be contained within the aims of A Rocha, and the following year, as the Trust began the process of acquiring a centre, they left the project. Shortly afterwards Les went to teach at the university at Faro. We have been grateful for the friendship that has continued and grown since then, and can now see how in fact God was leading us all to the work we eventually took up, but at the time it proved a painful disappointment. Surely, we felt, Christian teams shouldn't have to go through such misunderstandings and pain?

The puzzling thing is that if we had not worked together for the time we did, neither A Rocha nor Les and Wendy's later work in Faro could have come about, but there was little joy for any of us while we made up a team. In retrospect it is easy to see that the personality differences were so great that a joint project could never have worked out. But from the usual blend of extremely mixed raw material God managed in his wisdom to create things altogether more wonderful than we could have imagined. Given that we are so far from being ready for heaven, it is surprising it doesn't happen more often.

Meanwhile we carried on as a smaller team, and there was much to learn about the diverse and colourful village of Vila Verde if it was to be the place in which our future work would develop.

5

"I sent to the mayor, desiring the use of the town-hall. He refused, but the same day gave the use of it to a dancing-master." – John Wesley

Vila Verde is as near to a complete community as you can find in Europe at the end of the twentieth century. It could subsist quite happily without the help of any trade or service from anywhere else. There is a market, a stationer, a post office, a shoe-shop, two chemists, several motorbike repair shops, a terrible plumber and an excellent welder, good and bad cafés, a wonderful restaurant famous even in Lisbon for having no menu and for its chef who sleeps on the benches, a church (or two if you count the little one we have begun), a very fine baker, and several general stores. There are fish in the sea and shellfish in the estuary (although nothing like as many as there were even ten years ago), and there are good fields all around that yield everything anyone could reasonably wish to grow.

It seems as though every kind of person you can imagine lives in this one village. It is impossible to keep a secret in Vila Verde. People are given their public character early on in their lives. We once had some equipment stolen, and were told by Catarina that it was probably Coelho, now a corpulent Shake-spearean character in his late sixties, because she had never been able to trust him at school. The highest accolade awarded to anyone is that they are serious, perhaps reflecting P. G. Wodehouse's judgment: "lugubrious lot, the Portuguese". If

you ask anyone how things are going, the most effusive reply of all is *menos mal*, less badly. Certainly their former president, General Eanes, was never seen to smile once during his four-year tenure, thereby presumably reassuring the electorate. The current President, Mario Soares, is by comparison affable and relaxed, but is still regarded as serious because of his years in prison before the revolution.

Suffering is a great credential, and even I found my stock had risen once I had spent some weeks in hospital. The disadvantage was the succession of surgical scars which I had to inspect in the middle of conversations in the street – I was too English to present mine, but they have attracted admiring glances from the cognoscenti on the beach. The chemists are vital people in the community, as evidenced by there being two thriving businesses in a village of just over two thousand people, and serious money crosses their counters each day.

So we slowly came to know who was always drunk (that wasn't difficult), who was honest and who would cheat you, who was respected and who was thought to be mad. Inevitably in a community where everyone is watching everyone else, information is a valuable commodity, and not wasted on idle chat with newcomers, so mostly we found out the hard way. As it happened, however, almost the first family we met, Maria and Manuel and their children, grandchildren and great-grandchildren, proved to be absolutely serious, and one of the fulcral points of the village.

When we first arrived, we had a student friend with us, Alison Jewsbury, who came to help look after the children while Miranda worked on language study for a few hours every morning. She rented a room with Maria and Manuel, and so was the first in a long line of eventual A Rocha assistants to face their candid assessment. Maria has always taken their single status as a personal challenge, and comments freely and penetratingly on the respective merits of any boyfriends or girlfriends who are introduced to her. When they do not speak Portuguese this can usually be passed off as touching words of welcome, but Mark, who joined us later, always knew it was going to be a little tricky when he took Helen to meet Maria. Helen was doing a PhD on Camões and was well able to cope with Maria's powerful village accent, following perfectly Maria's unflinching catalogue of the relative attractions of previous pretenders to Mark's affections. She, and Mark by his account, had not realised there had been so many.

The great apple of Maria and Manuel's eye was Frank, O *Franco*, who only stayed with them for a few weeks, but whom they never forgot. Now there was a man with a proper appreciation of Portuguese beauty. And even beyond that, there was a man also who could eat as a man should, and not just pick at his food like so many disappointing English. He went on to work in the Afghan refugee camps on a forestry project, but they still hope he will return. Manuel drives a suicidal little moped with a high domed helmet settled provisionally on the top of his head, and if anything interesting happens within a radius of five miles, like road works or an accident, he finds his way there to observe within minutes. The whole family have a talent for the improbable that is hard to explain, but it reaches the heights with their granddaughter Gigi, who is studying cinema in Moscow and who has married a Colombian physicist.

Shortly after we settled into the flat in Vila Verde, we had our first experience of the problems that local conservationists were facing. A few kilometres to the east of the village, there was a marsh which, as we first saw it that spring, was alive with migrant waders. Collared Pratincoles hawked for dragonflies over the pools, and groups of Whimbrel working their way westwards along the coast dropped in for a few hours to feed and then moved on. There were Purple Herons and Little

Bitterns, Black Terns and Little Gulls, and the site was without equal for many miles of coastline in either direction. So we were appalled when we returned for a second visit a few weeks later and found red and white surveyors' marker poles dotted here and there all over the marsh. As the sad story slowly emerged in the local press during the next few weeks, we discovered that the area was to be drained in order to build a golf course. Despite being within the national ecological reserve by virtue of its proximity to the coast, all the necessary authorisation had been granted and so there was no way for anyone to prevent the site being irrevocably damaged. Portugal had yet to join the European Community, and so although what was planned was clearly illegal under European law, there was nothing to be done.

We discovered from friends living nearby that the development had been permitted because the government biologist employed by the developers to assess the area had produced a report saying the area was occasionally used by gulls and nothing else. Subsequently, when the dune system was breached and the golf course faced imminent salinisation, the work there was officially condemned as an example of destructive development, but by then the damage was done and the profits were made.

As we watched what happened on the marsh, and later at many other sites along the coast, we became increasingly aware that some of the forces that cause such environmental destruction are not morally or spiritually neutral. "The earth is defiled by its people, they have disobeyed the laws, violated the statutes and broken the everlasting covenant. Therefore a curse consumes the earth," says the prophet Isaiah, drawing the explicit connection between that particular form of abuse and rebellion against God.

We began to tell friends in the village of the plans we had for opening a centre for field studies by the estuary. "*Muito bonito* – very nice," they all said. "Of course you know all the land by the estuary has been sold to the Japanese, or was it the Germans, or perhaps it was the Dutch? Either way they're going to put in a golf course, and a lot of hotels, and there's talk of a marina." Having seen how fast a marsh could disappear, it all sounded horribly familiar. We had wanted to be somewhere where we could make a difference, but the future of the estuary looked far from certain. Once or twice we resorted to praying and fasting for the site at Alvor, because we were aware that the destruction of the earth matters to God, and it was not merely a question of competing economic priorities. Our growing appreciation of the vital importance to a whole range of species in the ecosystem gave us the conviction to oppose the casual but complete transformations that were imposed on them out of a desire for profit.

We soon discovered that in protecting the habitats of the Mediterranean, legislation in Brussels is of very little use unless someone can earth it all locally and become fully involved. Perhaps Christians are better equipped than many to understand this because they know that God sent Jesus as a man. They can understand from his life that suffering is the context for mission, not luxurious bureaucracy, and perhaps they have reasons for caring about the world around them that are powerful enough to keep them on site when few others will either stay, or go in the first place.

As we talked to people in Vila Verde about what we were hoping to do, we realised that some already understood the importance of the area in other ways apart from simply as something to be sold to foreigners. It would be well worth while to use a centre to provide opportunities for as many as possible in the area to consider it that way. Even so, it was only some years later, during a meeting about creating a nature reserve on the Alvor estuary, that the full force of the importance of local opinion came home. When the implications of the plan for the village began to be discussed, the emotional temperature suddenly rose. There were loud voices from the back of the hall, and the calm discussion was transformed into a violent argument. We hadn't said anything from the start, but from that point on even those who had come down from Lisbon were swept aside as outsiders, just as were the one or two who had come over from nearby towns. The only ones left with any credibility in the argument were those for whom Alvor was their *terra*, their own place. The right to contribute was earned by having lived there, and not by being important elsewhere. Jesus chose to be unimportant in Jerusalem or Rome in order to be in Galilee with the unimportant, and that is how mission will always be best conducted. It has also been of some consolation at times when we have felt most useless. "Well at least we are here," we have thought, "and if we weren't, there would be no one else for a few miles in each direction able to explain about Jesus, if anyone should ever want to know..."

This was the part of our work which was more easily

55

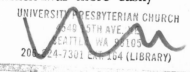

understood by many of those who were supporting A Rocha. As we slowly worked towards fluency, our aim was to gain an understanding of the local and national church and the different organisations that work within it in order to see what our contribution could be. This was not, however, the "Christian side" to our work. It was simply an important band in the spectrum of work to which we were called.

In Vila Verde there was no protestant church, but there were two in the nearby town of Portimão. The two pastors, one a Pentecostal and the other a Baptist, had never met each other although they had both been working in churches less than a kilometre apart for five years. It was our first introduction to the deep suspicion that existed between the different denominations, and seemed to be only one of the problems that the churches were facing.

We had been told that there were few other active Christians in our area. The Roman Catholic church, to which many people theoretically belonged, had in practice little influence over the way people thought and lived. Our local Roman Catholic bishop in Faro estimated that only 5 per cent of people in the Algarve were practising Catholics. In addition, few of those Catholic churches were giving a clear and biblical account of Christian belief to those who attended, which left the great majority living with a vacuum of half-held beliefs about the church and the priesthood, and a hazy notion of a distant God who was probably condemning them for being bad Catholics. The lessons from our early language study were borne out; although the Algarve has only one mosque, Islam has until recently been a powerful cultural influence. As hypermarkets and new businesses have mushroomed following Portugal's entry into the EC in 1986, so familiar Euro-ideas about happiness being a by-product of material prosperity, and morality being a matter of private conviction, have taken hold. Against this background, the protestant churches are numerically tiny and geographically very scattered. The Igreja Lusitana with which we as a family are associated is one of the smaller churches and has sixteen congregations in Portugal, none south of the Lisbon area. Frequently the pastors of many of the protestant denominations had no more than a few years of schooling, which made it difficult for them to communicate with the growing number of graduates and professional people. In the universities, evangelical students were normally outnumbered by almost a thousand to one.

The needs of the Christian world seemed as overwhelming as those of the conservation groups. We could only hope to help and support a few people even when we were well established, so it seemed sensible to concentrate our limited efforts in three areas: first, in student work, with Christians encouraging them to relate their beliefs to the rapidly changing society around them, but also with others to present a clear statement of the meaning of Christian belief; secondly, in building interdenominational bridges so that we could help out wherever we were asked; and thirdly, in establishing a local church among our friends and neighbours. Over the years we have probably done only the first, which was the easiest, halfway reasonably, but our intentions have remained the same as those we established at the beginning in Vila Verde.

We had not been living in Vila Verde for very long when Alan Pallister, whose educated commentary on our plans had made me miss the plane in Lisbon, invited us to help with a training camp run by the Grupo Bíblico Universitário, the Christian student movement that he was helping to lead. As so often happens, some of our closest friends in Portugal were made on that first occasion. Many of the students were very impressive. Alfredo Abreu was a young sociologist, from a family that like so many others had come back from Angola when Portugal had given up its colonies following the 1974 Revolution. For the first three years in Lisbon, he and eleven others lived in very basic conditions in three rooms while he carried on at school. In his final year, he won a scholarship to study in the USA, and it was there that he became a Christian. When we met him, he was still in his first year at Lisbon University, but was already outstandingly committed and thoughtful. Although Salazar's over-protective dictatorship became increasingly oppressive through the 1960s, one curious benefit was that its dark umbrella did serve to protect

Portuguese society from some of the more damaging aspects of the cultural upheavals that affected the rest of Europe. As a result, there are fewer signs of the divisions between the generations that are found in many other countries. Portuguese families remain very united, and many students seem to understand children very well. Alfredo was no exception, and he struck up a warm friendship with Joanna, Esther and Jeremy, as well as with us. Following the camp he came to stay a few times and before long we all felt he was almost part of our family.

The camp set a pattern for us, and in successive years we often travelled north from the Algarve in the week after Easter to help out. We could see that an A Rocha centre could be very helpful for small groups of students for their conferences, not least because the students always seem to get as much from being part of a family as from the more formal teaching sessions. The Benestad family, Norwegians working as student staff workers in Coimbra, have always opened their home to students for similar reasons. A couple of years ago when Alfredo also became a staff worker for the Grupo Bíblico Universitário, he and the other leaders incorporated this idea into the structure of the national camps. They have been organised as much for committed Christians as for others, and families have been invited to be available for groups of students during the camp. They have felt that there are few opportunities for students to get to know Christian families, and that the contemporary secular models of family life leave a lot to be desired. For our part, we have always felt that the definition of a family includes all the various people who pass through it at different times, and so the children as much as ourselves appreciate not being left as an isolated nucleus. The children frequently have more to give in uncomplicated affection and acceptance than we do, and they are the ones who usually provide the interest.

In trying to understand and be of service to the churches of the Algarve, we accepted every invitation, visited every church within fifty miles, and explained to every group that the eventual centre would be available for any activity that they wished to plan there. Later as time became absorbed in our own work we had to limit ourselves, but it was probably a useful start. It soon became clear that our contribution in the churches was always going to be limited unless we signed up as members of whatever denomination it was. Furthermore, many Catholic priests, in our area at least, regard Protestants as in the same camp as Mormons or Jehovah's Witnesses, and so there was no possibility of working together across that particular divide. Our local priest has proved to be a past master at accepting an invitation to lunch in principle, but not on any particular day – eight years have passed since the first friendly conversation, subsequently repeated at fairly regular intervals, and we're still waiting for him to come. Reciprocally, many protestant pastors believe the Roman Catholic church to be the Antichrist.

The first steps towards establishing a local church under the auspices of the Igreja Lusitana were very tentative indeed. Our landlords had welcomed us to the flat with a postcard that said "God Loves You" which seemed a promising start, and after a while we learned that they would be interested in reading the Bible with us from time to time. One or two other people in the village said the same, and so we looked around for somewhere to meet. So it was that the long and tortuous path to becoming a church began with some very damp occasions reading the Bible with friends and others on winter nights in the *Casa do Povo*, the People's House. It soon became apparent that given the disastrous state of the roof and the resultant heavy layer of condensation on the concrete floor, we were the only *Povo* foolish enough to want to use the building, which is probably why, in return for a modest donation to the local football team, we were allowed to meet there. Our efforts to move to a more comfortable room elsewhere (anywhere!) met with months of inscrutable delay that can only be truly appreciated by the postgraduate student of bureaucracy. I discovered committees in Portimão of whose existence the normal citizen might only dream, and filled in triplicate forms of Dickensian aspect in dusty waiting-rooms, but all to no avail.

It was not until a couple of years later, when the A Rocha centre was finally open, and the local council wished to bring one of its schools round, that the official doors opened on oiled hinges and we were suddenly able to use a fine modern room in the local council house for our monthly Sunday service. Nine years after we first met, our core group numbers around twelve ladies, plus some children and Manuel who by virtue of his age is considered an honorary lady anyway. Another twenty or so have come from time to time. In our defence I have to say that for most Portuguese towns that is a reasonable sized protestant church, and in Yemeni terms it would be a revival. Either way that's where we are. We have often thought that we have not so much planted a church as dug a hole where in time one might be planted. It does nothing to take away the deep joy we feel about Idalina, with whom Miranda has spent many hours over the years and who has a remarkably transformed life and extraordinary trust in God despite crippling arthritis and other real difficulties in her life. None of us understands why she seems to be the only one to be greatly changed, but it is certainly enough.

It is tempting to paint a colourful Mediterranean picture in the style of *My Family and Other Animals* and to depict Vila Verde as a happy community basking in the golden southern sun, cheerfully tolerant of their neighbours' foibles. There are many times when it comes very close to being true, on a Saturday morning in the market for example when everyone is out on the street and there are stories to tell and a lot of laughter. Manuel the baker (as opposed to any other of more than a hundred possible Manuels) throws in some extra rolls with the bread, and the children are happily occupied scrounging tangerines from a series of people on the fruit stalls. Sometimes we feel we have lived here all our lives, and will never be happy anywhere else.

However, there is another side to the village, the sad reality of fractured relationships, dark family feuds going back generations, the strange tendency for neighbours to make each other's life difficult if they can. Apparently it is a well-known feature of village life, but we have never fully understood it.

One of Miranda's friends, Lucília, has an orange orchard near the village. For the last five years she has never known from one day to the next if she can get to water it, because it

60

means crossing five yards of her neighbour's land, and the access is in dispute. At one point three years ago the tribunal ruled in her favour, but for the last two years they have been waiting for the appeal to be heard. Meanwhile she and her neighbour see each other nearly every day.

At different moments we have encountered these problems too, and they can bring much pain to all concerned. In our own case we were soon blamed by two large landowners because they were unable to gain permission to urbanise the farmland on the shores of the estuary. In the early days when we were primarily a foreign organisation, we didn't feel we should campaign for the protection of the area and its habitats, but our studies were always cited by Portuguese conservationists and the press when the discussion was raging. Later, soon after the centre opened, we found that illegal orders had been given to cut off our water supply because it crossed the neighbours' land, and the early friendly welcome from both of them was gone. A series of trivial but damaging episodes followed.

It is always difficult to live closely with people who hate what you are doing, and not to return the hostility, and we haven't always managed to shrug it off. It has helped us to understand the difficulties so many of our friends seem to have with others they know. In a large city it is easier to keep at a distance from those who wish to harm you, but at close quarters it makes Jesus's command to love your enemies very practical and uncomfortably difficult. If you see someone nearly every day, it is hard to recognise that what you are doing is going to be unwelcome to them, even if you believe it to be right.

It is impossible to work on environmental issues, particularly in somewhere like the Algarve, and not be involved in controversy, and of course it is equally impossible to be right every time in the positions you adopt. Chris Patten's comment about politics could equally well apply to conservationists: "When politicians begin to suggest that what they do and what they think are sanctified by universal truth, the wise man looks at the train times to the next town." We cannot always be right, and we cannot expect everyone to agree with what we suggest. Christian organisations trying to work in these controversial areas will make themselves unpopular at times, and we just have to learn the lessons of the Sermon on the Mount early on so that we can limit the damage and not respond in kind.

We are working in nature protection because we care about it more than about many other things, and so it isn't possible to be dispassionate when hunters with guns go through our garden, or when we meet a trapper with a plastic bag full of Stonechats, Black Redstarts and Meadow Pipits, some of which we have ringed in previous years, or when a reedbed we know to be a rare and wonderful site for migrants is needlessly drained or burnt. Recently, in order to teach the village an obscure lesson, our priest gave orders to wire in the colony of a hundred or so sparrows that have always nested in an outside space in the church roof. We were asked to go to reason with him, but the discussion was less than a meeting of minds. After two days during which the birds flew hopelessly at the netting, watched by many of our appalled friends, they finally succumbed. Only the different wisdom we find in Christ

can cope with the sense of outrage and anger and channel it into something that reflects his character and not our frustration. Judgment on the people involved is his to make, and not ours. We can only comment on the effect of what has been done, and if anything can still be salvaged, we can suggest what might be done to restore the value of the creation. To counter one form of destruction with another is of no help at all.

What I have often found hardest is the sense of powerlessness, of being without recourse to reason or justice, but this has been precisely the experience of everyone who has gone down the road Jesus took, establishing a different kingdom not based on force. There is always the possibility that the immediate battle will be lost in favour of winning a wider war that is defined quite differently, by eternal criteria. In our life and experience it goes without saying that what has been at stake has always been relatively unimportant, and the cost to ourselves insignificant. This cannot be said for many Christians all over the world, such as those in the refugee camps on the Thai border or in the prohibited churches of China. Their witness in the face of injustice and suffering is a powerful testimony to the greater power of God.

6

"You are, of course, looking for a little corner of Paradise..." – *letter from Bob Pullan*

The leaves on the almond trees opposite our flat in Vila Verde shrivelled to russet brown as the heat of the summer began in earnest. Very rapidly the flowers in the orchard burned out in the fierce sun, and we were not sorry to leave the stifling flat and to head north for a six-week language course in Coimbra. The beautiful city with its steep streets clustered below the old university on the top of the hill was a world away from the Moorish Algarve, and the opportunity to give some uninterrupted time to language study was very welcome. Even so, life was not without its moments of excitement.

Before we arrived, we had asked Øivind and Tone Benestad if they knew of anywhere we could rent while we did the course. They had found an amazing old balustraded house outside the city, almost buried in creepers behind, and with a façade of faded splendour; one half of it was available to rent. A family were living in the other half and would be happy to let us practise our Portuguese on them at any time. We were delighted by the arrangement, and Jo, Esther and Jeremy really enjoyed having the run of the large garden. Apart from the danger that they would disappear without trace into one of the deep ponds whose crust of vivid green algae made them seem like small lawns, it seemed ideal. It was while they were exploring on the first afternoon that they made an interesting discovery. "Mummy, quick, come and see! There's a lady living in a shed in the garden!" Yet again it seemed as though we had displaced our landlady, but this time it was to prove even more complicated.

A couple of nights later there were screams and yells from one of the upstairs windows, and simultaneously the downstairs shutters were shaken by a series of violent blows. A moment later the back door burst open, and a man brandishing an ivory stick came charging into the kitchen. The abuse he was yelling would definitely have been classified as extra-curricular by the university, so we hadn't a clue what was going on. He dashed past us and up the stairs into the bedroom where Jo and Esther were sleeping. We assumed he was a maniac intent on murdering the children, and rushed in there after him only to discover that our landlady had taken cover behind one of the beds. We alternated between trying to protect her and guarding the children, but after a brief mêlée during which he managed to land some blows on the screaming woman, there was the sound of sirens and he rushed out again. As we regained our breath and found some antiseptic for the cuts and bruises on our landlady's forehead and arms, we discovered that the children had slept soundly through it all. Life in Coimbra was obviously not going to be the academic idyll that we had been expecting.

It transpired that he was her estranged husband, and that these episodes were fairly frequent, which was why the family next door had phoned the police when they heard the beginnings of the argument. This time he had taken exception to her letting the house without consulting him. Clearly renting property in Portugal could be an unpredictable affair, and we resolved to talk to the neighbours before we rented a house next time.

Despite the drama, the house was a great favourite with all the family, and it proved stimulating to be back in contact with students again. Thus we returned a little reluctantly to the Algarve.

"If only we could find a property like that for sale around here," I said to Miranda as we puzzled over the problem yet again on our first evening back in the flat. We felt that after a full year in Portugal we were ready to move on to the challenge of opening a centre, but we were beginning to wonder if we would ever manage to find a suitable place. It was becoming clear that a minor miracle would be needed.

There were plenty of modern, marble-floored villas for sale in the Algarve, but we really needed a big, old house with plenty of space. The few houses we had seen which seemed suitable had invariably been in the family for years and were not for sale. There were plenty of derelict old cottages in the countryside, and quite a few big old houses in the towns, but nothing much in between. Furthermore, the house would need to be somewhere with enough interest to sustain field studies throughout the year. Most inland areas were burned out and dry for many months of the summer, and there would be little for visitors to do. Nearer the coast the habitats were limited, or the bulldozers were already moving in. We didn't want to add to the number of new buildings that were going up everywhere around us by starting from scratch and occupying yet more farmland. It was a consolation to know that a lot of people were praying that we would find somewhere, and with every passing day we were more sure that this was the only way out of the impasse.

As we considered the problem, we could think of only two large houses near the shores of the estuary. One belonged to Sr Duarte, and had been in the family since the eighteenth century. He would hardly want to sell, and even if he did, the house was too far from the railway station and road where most of the eventual visitors to the centre would arrive. The other, Cruzinha, meaning Little Cross, was ideally placed on a slight rise halfway down the main track from the village to the shore. It was a beautiful house simply constructed around an old high-roofed cottage. Around the house there were two acres of olive and almond trees, together with some pines and acacias. I had talked to the owners once, when they were visiting from Lisbon, and had walked around its spacious rooms on the cool tile floors, but they had told me that they had no plans to sell the house, which they had converted themselves fifteen years ago. In recent years they had rented it out very profitably. Nevertheless, they had liked the idea of the house being used as a field study centre. "If we ever decide to sell, you'll be the first to know," they said. Miranda had never forgotten the place either. She first saw it after we had been to look at a ruined cottage nearby, during our first weeks in Portugal. She wrote in her journal, "The cottage would need too much work, and we were pretty discouraged – but what about Cruzinha?"

Since I had been shown round, we had never seen Cruzinha's owners again, so I was surprised to find them waiting at the bus-stop in the village a few days after we returned from Coimbra. When I asked them about the house I was even more surprised to hear that while we had been away they had decided to put it on the market. Several prospective buyers had already been to look round. That afternoon I went in to the estate agents in Portimão, and was astonished to discover how little was being asked for the house. They were obviously hoping for a quick sale. So began several months of tension more acute than we have ever experienced before or since. Almost every day it seemed we encountered different people driving down to look at the house in discouragingly wealthy looking cars, and the rumours among our neighbours agreed that the property was a bargain that would be sold any day.

Cruzinha needed a lot of work doing on it, but when we had the surveyor's report, it confirmed the local opinions. Even so, our own decision had to be made more slowly. The Trust had never wanted to accumulate capital before we had a property in view, and so we had to start from scratch. At the time even the current account held little more than a hundred pounds, and there had been some difficult moments in the previous few months as the total dipped dangerously near the red. However, Bob Pullan was prepared to allow A Rocha to disrupt his life yet again and came out at short notice to see Cruzinha. He liked what he saw, and following his visit the Trustees agreed to write to all our supporters to tell them about the house, giving three weeks for replies to come in from those who wanted to help.

Through all the uncertainty Bob's letters were full of the language of faith: "So we are to sweat it out for three weeks and possibly longer. Have courage that if the Lord wants us to have the building and land soon he will keep it for us. If not, then we shall find ourselves owning it in two to three years' time . . ." After three weeks were up less than half the money had come in, and the Trustees felt that we had done all we could. They had heard from Les and Wendy that they too were unconvinced by the idea, and they were no longer sure that Cruzinha could be bought. Bob wrote sadly:

> It is not crystal clear to any of the Trustees that the Lord wishes us to have Cruzinha now – if we are not seeing clear signs, he will be patient with us. There is much more I would want to say to you in comfort and encouragement. It seems the business of the Trust will bring hard lessons but our Lord Jesus has promised us that he will not forsake us.

However, the Trustees could not know as certainly as we did that we could hardly have expected more from a letter to our supporters. Many of them were our friends and we knew that they were as broke as we were. To us, the amount they had promised seemed nothing short of miraculous, and we felt sure that if only we could explain what A Rocha was planning to people who we knew sometimes helped to fund Christian projects, then the rest of the money would be provided.

On the one occasion when we seriously wavered, and buying the house began to seem completely impossible, we were able to draw on the faith of others who were more distant from the pressures of the situation than either we or the Trustees were. I drove out to a hotel not far from the flat in Vila Verde to phone Charlie and Anita. We knew that they and the church in Cranham had been praying. "Perhaps we are being unwise? Do you really think this is possible?" I asked. "Maybe we shouldn't be so attached to this particular place?" They were in no doubt. "You will have the house, and you mustn't give up now. We'll get the church to pray." We knew that the supporting churches on Merseyside were praying too, and as they did so, our confidence that the house would belong to A Rocha began to grow again. It is hard to explain such convictions, and ours have certainly not proved infallible, but on this occasion we felt sure of God's leading and certain that it should be pursued to the end.

I am ashamed now of the way I badgered the Trustees to let me come back to England for two weeks, and of the way that once I was at large on the motorways in a borrowed car I cornered friends and relations to give us ideas for people I could talk to about Cruzinha. Wilfred and Heather Dyer, who had visited us in Vila Verde while on holiday nearby, had helped a lot by phoning round and fixing the first appointments. My little set of photographs of the house became gradually more dog-eared as they were produced several times each day, and I discovered that it was customary on such ventures to have a smoothly laid out colour-printed leaflet with a persuasive text to leave with people. My parents and Alan and Kerry Ritchie allowed me to monopolise their phones, and Bob lent me his car so that I could get to four Merseyside churches in a morning.

It all generated far too much pressure for everyone concerned, but the problem was that by now we cared about it too much to be cool and dispassionate. We as a family were now at the point where the difficulties were compounding themselves, and it was taking all the faith we had to stay with what we believed. In the same week that we discovered that Cruzinha was for sale, Oscar had come up to the flat to explain that he wanted their home back. This seemed entirely reasonable, considering that he had never been consulted by Isabel

before she decided to let it. We couldn't easily stay there anyway, as by now Miranda was expecting a baby, and there was
no space in the tiny flat to put a carrycot, let alone another
bed. We had walked around every street in the village and
talked to everyone we knew, but could find nowhere else to
stay. A few days before I went back to England, we had moved
to a rented house as near to Cruzinha as we could find. Even
so it was twenty minutes' drive away (or forty if the three level
crossings were against us). It was on the same estate as Tom
and Edite, which was a great comfort because by now Miranda
was feeling as unwell as she usually did during pregnancy. She
has always had an unusual gift of faith, however, and remained
unshaken through all the highs and lows of the following few
days. One consolation was that we were finally able to get our
belongings out of store following the appeal against the refusal
of our residence permit, and we particularly enjoyed the
Christmas cake that had been thrown into the luggage by kind
friends at the last minute before we left Upton. They had had
the foresight to lace it with rum, so it emerged a year and a
half later even better than it had gone in.

Very occasionally events become a little Technicolor as God
heightens our perceptions to make things more clear than
usual. During the fortnight in England a pattern began to
emerge and I was frequently astonished as very unpromising
conversations suddenly swung and people who had been
showing only polite interest decided that after all they would
support the project. It was clear that something was going on
well out of my control, and after a while I began to enjoy the
experience. I rapidly began to learn things about the surprising
world of Christian funding where it can be more important to
spend a day with an elderly lady who can give only fifty pounds
but who decides to pray, than half an hour with a wealthy man
who might seem to be a more relevant person to talk to. The
wealthy Christians I did meet constantly surprised me. One or
two lived very simply but administered hundreds of thousands
of pounds, doing all they could to discover how God wished
it to be spent. I had never appreciated what a difficult vocation
it could be to enable Christian work by giving money away,

and I became aware of how important it is to keep complete integrity where money is involved. "Follow the money" was the advice given to Bob Woodward in *All the President's Men*, and it is a path that often leads to the truth about Christian organisations too. At times it was difficult to resist the temptation to tailor the description of A Rocha to suit a particular conversation. Every person I approached had different interests which they wanted to support, and few of them had ever supported anything like A Rocha before, so I decided never to ask for money but simply to explain what the Trust wanted to do with the house, leaving the decisions with the different people I met, and the outcome to God.

Meanwhile I heard from Miranda that the chances of the house remaining unsold were daily becoming more slim. The tenants had reached saturation point with so many people coming to see the house and were refusing to show prospective buyers around any more. My two weeks of travelling ended, and I returned to Portugal to await the outcome of the Trustees' meeting the following Saturday. With a final gift on the morning that they met to make their decision, the total was still five thousand pounds short of the asking price. Bob's letter to us recorded the outcome:

> We prayed twice. It was David Ager who quietly said that he thought that what the Lord had done was to give us enough. We phoned the owner, but he was out so we disbanded with Alan looking at a second-hand car, and David to phone Portugal later. He told me at about 10.30 p.m. that we had the house with no demurring from the owner. I had worked on the Bird Report on the train coming home to Upton, and I was suddenly transformed from a very weary middle-aged man to a renewed person. On Sunday morning there was a communion service and we told a few people as we went in but it was introduced in the prayers. I could see the happiness in the faces as I watched the A Rocha supporters coming down the aisle – others were similarly moved. It has been a wonderful thing for each of them to know what a great and faithful Lord we have and to know his very

positive confirmation that Cruzinha is right. I do so wish you could have been there for I know a little of how you have suffered and felt frustrated over the past weeks. It is clear to me that this was the way to do it, for otherwise the involvement of so many others would have been much less. When I phoned the churches in the afternoon and late morning I had the same response of initial unbelief and then an outpouring of thanks and praise to God. I pray we can all be worthy of his trust in the future months and years.

We discovered some months later that our offer was neither the first nor the highest. A fortnight before the Trustees agreed the sale, a Dutch family had given a deposit for the property to their estate agent. He had, however, decided to delay contacting the owners for reasons that we have never fully understood, during which time our own deposit reached the owners. It is a relief to know the family now as friends and to have heard them say that they feel the house is better used by the Trust than it could ever have been as their holiday home. Each year they call in, often with friends, to see how the project is progressing, and to explain almost with pride their unorthodox part in its story.

In the middle of all the decisions about Cruzinha, we had received a letter from a student at Cambridge, Mark Bolton. It was short and to the point. "I am graduating in zoology this summer, and have heard about A Rocha through my home church in Reading. I am a committed Christian and a keen birder. Would there be any chance of a job?" Once we had met Mark there was no doubt that there would be. He proved to be a gift to the project and set a pattern for successive generations of assistant wardens by his commitment to professional field work, and the unfailing cheerfulness with which he met the unexpected demands that seem to be the hallmark of work for A Rocha. We had hoped to be at Cruzinha by the time he arrived, and were planning to rent the house near Tom and Edite for only a few months, but of course things took a lot longer than that, and so Mark rented the room from Maria and Manuel, unaware that with it came a close interest in his social life ... He came over to our estate on his motor-bike each weekend to stay with us, frequently getting soaked in the pouring rain of his first winter. We didn't have a spare room, and so he slept on the sofa in the living room, tolerantly accepting the avalanche of Harris children that poured on to his bed in the morning.

After the dramatic days of the sale, the following six months were somewhat of an anti-climax. The paperwork dragged on and the transfer of Cruzinha was delayed by a series of bureaucratic problems. One particularly discouraging morning I happened to meet the estate agent who had dealt with the Dutch family in Portimão. "Where are you living these days? Oh still in Lagôa. Well I'm not surprised, you'll never own that house," he said. "It's a legal impossibility." But by now we were beginning to gain an appetite for impossibilities, and as time went on we saw that the dream was about to become a reality. The delay was far from a waste of time as it gave us space as a family and as a team which we badly needed after all the uncertainties and moves of the previous months. It is a wonderful thing to be able to work together as a family and in close association with other people, but it implies that you have to be sufficiently sorted out to take on extra demands at inconvenient moments. It is impossible to put on a public face to cover private disarray for very long, and it takes time to develop the genuine qualities of relationship and trust that are needed. We were already finding that we had many visitors both staying and calling in as word of A Rocha began to spread. That summer they camped in the tiny garden of our rented house, and slept on the flat roof. Many Sundays we convened impromptu worship. It seemed as though the hospitality of A Rocha was beginning whether we had a centre ready or not.

Among the frequent callers were David and Simone Rees. We had first met them in Vila Verde when they were trying to find their way to a plant nursery nearby where David had an interview. Their enthusiasm for plants was matched only by their knowledgeable curiosity about everything else that grew or crawled or flew, and we soon found that we had a lot to talk about. They had recently decided to follow up a growing

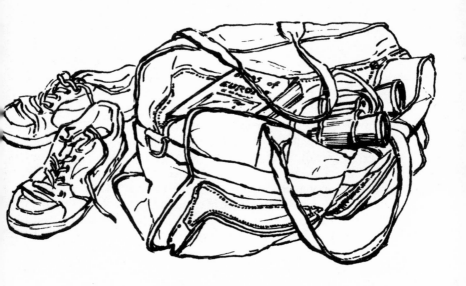

conviction that the Christian faith needed closer examination. During the months at Lagôa we were able to meet each week to study the Bible and pray together, and we could see how important the time was to us all. Even so none of us imagined that within a few years their family would be at the heart of a thriving international church near Faro, established over the next few years by another couple, Peter and Marianne Sluimer, who like us had been helped to settle in the Algarve by Tom and Edite.

We were also glad of a pause in A Rocha's progress, because at the beginning of the long hot summer Bethan was born. There were some nervous moments in the final weeks. Miranda had been going for check-ups to a consultant in Portimão, but as the delivery date drew closer he began to mutter cryptically that all was not well. We both went to see him to try to discover why, and to find out what we should do about it, but he would not be drawn any further beyond saying that Miranda should go for tests in Faro the following weekend. By then there were only three weeks to go and so instead she decided to invest in a bus ticket to Lisbon to get a second opinion. As a first visit to the capital city it proved eventful. There was indeed a problem, and for the safety of the baby she was advised to stay and to be closely monitored. An additional stipulation was that she should eat as many sweet buns and cakes as possible; at least, that was the version that reached the Algarve. At the end of the week, to our great relief, Bethan was prematurely but safely delivered, looking a little shrivelled, particularly around the knees I recall, but completely fit.

When I took the rest of the family up to Lisbon in the Red Rose to meet their new sister, we discovered that because Ronald Reagan was in town the American security services had taken over every available bed. We spent the night stacked into what appeared to be a condemned building near the Praça Marquês de Pombal. When we went to the hospital the following morning, Jeremy held Bethan very tightly and then said thoughtfully, "When it's bigger, it *might* be a boy . . ."

7

"I am of my otes it is this wurk I know it will bring me to deaths door i know it will ..." – William Penrose Taplow

In autumn the thoughts of the birder lightly turn to migration, and so at 3.30 a.m. on many mornings from late August onwards I wheeled my motorbike quietly down the road, started it out of earshot of the house and set off inland to a farm where two British ornithologists, Ralph and Glenis Vowles, were ringing migratory birds. Ringing is a highly skilled operation, and I had never had time in England to embark on the thorough training that was necessary. We had realised early on that it would be very useful to be able to ring birds as part of A Rocha's work, not just for the data it would provide, but also as an activity for visitors to help with. The fascination of seeing birds at close quarters for the first time, or of handling a bird bearing a ring from thousands of kilo-metres away, is one of the highlights for many visitors to a bird observatory. It seemed as though it would be some months before we could begin work on Cruzinha, so Ralph and Glenis's offer of training could hardly have been better timed.

At the farm, birds were caught in fine mist nets, and a num-bered ring was carefully fitted to the leg. The details were then recorded and if the bird was captured or found elsewhere, the route of its migration could be discovered. There was one practical snag; in order to be ready for the first birds to move in the early morning, the luckless trainee had to have the nets up before dawn, and the journey to the ringing site through the freezing night air was often eventful. The bike had a highly idiosyncratic water cooling system with a penchant for cutting out the engine for enforced rests in the more remote valleys near the *serra*. I was always aware that this might happen just as I went past one of the other farms where the dogs had discovered that my regular appearance could be counted on to enliven the long night hours. As the weeks passed they developed some decidedly sophisticated techniques for effective ambush, but they seemed to be satisfied by a few lunges at my trouser legs and a race with the bike, so I survived the autumn more or less intact. By early November when the rains came and put paid to any further ringing, I had handled over a thousand birds and was reckoned to be competent to start some limited ringing on my own account without causing undue harassment to the Algarve's migrants.

It was around that time that we had the first signs of the next approaching storm, but it had nothing to do with these nocturnal adventures. I began to feel distinctly unwell on the hotter days, and was sleeping very badly. We put it down to general stress and decided to check with the mission doctors when we next went on leave. Mark and I continued with field work and finally in January 1986 the owners consented to allow the builders to go into Cruzinha and start on the alterations, although the sale was far from complete and it was still impossible to exchange contracts. We were able to work only a little at a time as the money came in to the Trust, and it took over a year to install water, electricity and gas and make the place generally habitable. Mark and I spent weeks painting, remembering how initially Ronald Lockley had also been able to give only half an eye to the phenomenon of migration as he put the observatory buildings in order on Skokholm.

We could see there was much to learn about the area. The marshes were often visited by local hunters but even so the number of waders was impressive. Each different habitat on the two-kilometre peninsula reaching down from Vila Verde between the two estuaries of the Alvor and the Farelo needed careful study. Even in winter there were Hoopoes and White Storks, absent from much of the rest of Europe at that time of the year, while on the estuary itself a few Caspian Terns could be found with the numerous Sandwich Terns and gulls. We were impatient to begin regular surveys, but the work to do on the house seemed to be endless.

The big question every day was whether Zé Manuel, a builder from the village who had agreed to help, would turn up with his mate. He seemed to know by extra-sensory perception if we were going to be away on field work, and if so he would go off to another site, so we had no alternative but to keep going ourselves. These were the days of the Algarve building boom, and there was a huge amount of work for everyone, so finding a plumber or a carpenter with time to take on new work was virtually impossible. Zé Manuel had a wonderfully optimistic attitude to construction. What did it matter if the ceiling of a corridor worked out around waist high? A little lower than could be wished for, certainly, but with a little goodwill on both sides and some bending of the waist one could pass, couldn't one? What matters is sincerity.

I made the mistake of going to Lisbon one weekend to speak at a conference and returned to find a fine external staircase built across a couple of windows. One could still see out? Good. And how useful if the children should wish to come in by a different door. And the important thing is that we are all friends, working on this job together with seriousness. Actually, he was right. We moved the staircase, though, despite a strong impulse to leave it. To an architect the Algarve must seem one of the great unexplored territories, full of startling and original moments.

"I'll move in to Cruzinha when there is running water, but not before," Miranda said, with long experience of the inconvenience that my optimism has frequently brought to our married life. As the only stipulation she made about the water was that it should run, we moved in to Cruzinha on Maundy Thursday 1986. Soon after we arrived, Miranda disappeared to organise the first nappy change, and I waited a little apprehensively for the discovery that I knew was to follow. "This water is bright red!" she shouted from the bathroom, a note of betrayal in her voice. It was obviously time to check something urgent at the other end of the house.

The muddy water remained a vivid colour for some weeks while the disused borehole cleared itself, but at least it ran. A few other things were missing, but their absence was carried off by Zé Manuel's evident pride at his handiwork. The pièce de résistance was a designer towel rail in marble, fortunately cheaper than the imported plastic equivalent. It graced the bathroom which unavoidably had no glass in the windows.

From the first the house was open to visitors. We moved in downstairs while the upstairs flat was completed, and so became very used to the constant stream of people in and out. The first two were there when we arrived with the removal van. "Ah, just moving in, are you?" they enquired politely. "That's good. Actually," they continued, "it's very good timing, because we need your help. Where around here can you find Mirror Orchids?" Mark pored over the map with them as we carried rugs and boxes past, and then they drifted off.

In the first week we counted seventy different visitors who had come for a variety of reasons but mostly looking for Ocellated Lizards, or for information on where to find Spectacled Warblers, or on Sunday to join us for worship. We found it all exhilarating if a little hair-raising at times. We began to witness for the first time something which we have seen on innumerable occasions since, a change that can come over those who remain here for a while. When we had first taken over the house with the builders, the place had a completely different atmosphere. On our first evening as residents, at something like two in the morning with piles of books for the library and furniture in heaps all around, we prayed that God's Spirit would move in with us to every room. From that moment we all sensed a difference in the feel of the place. It comes as no surprise now when visitors break off from asking about birds and say, "This house is very peaceful, isn't it?" We know it is and we know why, and we are well aware that it is certainly nothing to do with those of us who are working here who can have bad days like anyone else. It is more also than the beautiful setting of the house, because that was always there.

Any Christian project has its unseen dynamics, and we are no exception. From the very earliest days of the church, spiritual opposition has been a reality that Christians have had to reckon with. As C. S. Lewis so famously explained in *The Screwtape Letters*, there seem to be two equal and opposite errors to avoid if we are to understand what is going on. The first error is to assume that such an antiquated and mythological notion as a Devil who attacks the work of Christians has no place in enlightened modern thinking. However, we are not at liberty to believe any differently from Jesus if we are his disciples, and he was in no doubt that we have an enemy. We can see his true character in the suffering of Cambodia or Croatia, or even in the wreckage of a car smash.

The second error is to lay all difficulty at Satan's door, so that our lives are given significance by being played out as a cosmic drama for which we can take little responsibility. From the early days of arriving in Portugal we were aware that we were experiencing a different level of disruption from that which we had met in the more sheltered environment of a praying church on Merseyside. There were days when we felt abnormally discouraged, dejected beyond all reason at the prospect of continuing with A Rocha. Sometimes everything we did seemed to be trivially but recognisably disrupted. After a while we came to understand more readily what was happening, to depend on praying a little more, and to be aware that we were very dependent on the prayers of others to overcome problems that would not be shifted in any other way. The Trustees in the UK had from time to time experienced the same thing and there was a need to be constantly watchful on each other's behalf. So when we went back to England on leave that July, and I spoke to the doctor about how tired I felt, it didn't come as a complete surprise to be told after some tests that I had developed sizeable tumours in my adrenal glands which would require major surgery.

"Rare as hen's teeth," said the surgeon cheerfully, perhaps intending to couch the news in suitably ornithological terms for me to understand. I'm afraid I was a disappointment.

"I've never heard of them," I said, seeing a rapid return to Cruzinha drifting away from me as the prospect of weeks in hospital began to sink in. "What are they?"

"I don't know," he said. I began to think that by comparison prising information out of the gynaecologists in Portimão was relatively easy. "I suppose that's because they're so rare. I was hoping you could tell me."

Teeth or no teeth, and adrenal glands (or to be precise, no adrenal glands), the outcome was that our return to Portugal had to be delayed by another four months.

Mark was left with the daunting prospect of continuing to hold the fort on his own. David and Dora Glass, a remarkable Anglo-Brazilian couple with many years of overseas experience behind them, had helped him in the summer and could return for part of the time. They had made an enormous impression on many of our neighbours in their short stay, and their particular concern for people who are living in real poverty brought them very close to many of our friends nearby. "Dona Dora" still has almost legendary status nearly seven years later. Fortunately they were used to fairly provisional living conditions, and David was a past master at improvising and fixing. Never had the Red Rose run so sweetly as when under his care.

But for much of the autumn and winter Mark was living at Cruzinha alone. The builders were still on site, and there were often many visitors, but he decided to go ahead with an ambitious project to map the winter distribution of the birds of the Western Algarve, to be published in atlas form. The field work involved spending six hours in each of thirty-one eight-by ten-kilometre quadrats. Luckily it was a particularly fine winter, but even so he had some interesting moments in some of the more remote areas.

Early one winter morning he was crossing a shallow river behind a beach on the west coast when he walked into an area of quicksand. In a few seconds he was sinking fast, and every time he tried to lift one leg he went in further. As it happened, a few weeks before he had been given a book for Christmas by a thoughtful aunt. It was entitled *A Thousand and One Useful Things to Know*, and number five hundred and sixty-three was "How to Get Out of Quicksand" (you Lie Down Flat and Roll Over – I pass it on for free). I hope his aunt will forgive me if I say that it is unlikely that Mark would have studied the book so carefully had he not foolishly agreed to accompany a youth group on a bus from Faro to Utrecht over the New Year (faithfully following the policy of agreeing to every request on principle). To while away the interminable journey, and to distract himself from the numbing cold as they crossed the mountains of Spain, he delved deeply into the mysteries and engraved the words of wisdom on his mind, so when he found himself in a real quicksand he was well equipped. Apparently the worst thing was lying back into the river, but as he did so, his legs slowly began to surface, and after a nerve-racking moment or two he was able to crawl out on to firmer ground.

When the atlas was produced later in the year it contained some thirty of Mark's drawings, and the first edition fairly rapidly sold out. We celebrated its publication with seafood rice at our local café, but soon learned that this was a mistake. Never take a zoologist out for seafood rice unless you wish to learn about untold submarine horrors, and spend much of the meal dissecting and identifying. Stick to chicken and chips.

In our absence Mark was also able to welcome the first Portuguese birders to the centre. He wrote to the Trustees in August:

The real highlight for me was the (premature and therefore unexpected!) arrival of our very first Portuguese birders, Henrique who I had met in Évora, and Carlos. They stayed four days and gave a hand with digging the pond and other jobs. On their final day we left at 5.00 a.m. for Cape St Vincent for some dawn seabird watching and to see if raptor migration had started yet. Good views of Cory's and Balearic Shearwaters – new birds for both of them – and then Black Kite and Montagu's Harrier. Lunch in the café at Sagres and then off to Monchique to look for Azure-winged Magpies and Rock Buntings. Here the results of the winter and breeding bird surveys paid dividends – I knew exactly where we were likely to find both species and so we were not disappointed – and then back to Cruzinha for dinner. After a communal meal, amongst the dirty dishes, we began to discuss the origins of A Rocha, the Christian background, the reasons for Christians setting up a bird observatory and why in Portugal, the differences between Protestants and

Catholics, the creation evolution debate, the big bang theory, the claims of Jesus Christ. We did some Bible reading and before we knew where we were it was 1 a.m. – the washing up had to wait to the following morning.

We knew that there were probably only about forty active birdwatchers in the country, one for every six thousand hunters apparently, and so these were good days. Carlos and Henrique also introduced us to a common feature of such visits; we rarely had any warning, and it would be difficult to get much sleep. In part this was due to the infamous Ghost Train on which many of the students opted to arrive which travelled apparently without a schedule across the plains of the Alentejo from Évora, arriving at any time between midnight and 2 a.m. Combining such a different perception of time with that of our meticulously organised British visitors, who had usually booked months in advance and fretted at a five-minute delay at the level crossing lest we should think them late, was quite a challenge. Fortunately we had plenty of floor space and several tents, so no one was ever turned away.

In early January we finally returned to Cruzinha from our extended stay on Merseyside. All the building work upstairs had been completed, with David using the date of our return as an incentive to galvanise Zé Manuel, so after a few days we could move our stuff upstairs and free the visitors'

accommodation. The day of the move itself was eventful because by then I was minus a couple of ribs, and still adjusting to life on maintenance steroids. The doctors had explained that if ever I contracted a stomach bug, I would have to take the steroids by injection. Within moments of waking up on the morning of the move I was violently sick. We had some supplies, but as it was the beginning of the weekend Miranda decided to head for Portimão to track down some more. Failing to find the necessary phials at the hospital, she scoured the various pharmacies in the pouring rain for extra supplies of injectable hydrocortisone, before she was eventually given some by a local army doctor. By the time the fateful moment came to do what any self-respecting diabetic does without a qualm, I was in a poor state and was shaking too severely to have much hope of success. Miranda took over, having first remembered the advice from the hospital to practise on an orange, which I must confess was only marginally reassuring for her, and decidedly intimidating for me.

Once the deed was done, I recovered rapidly from the shakes, considerably helped by the sound of a blast of "Colonel Bogey" from the horn of Zé Manuel's lorry which came roaring down the drive to the house with his mate in the cab. "We have come," he announced, "to celebrate the return of Senhor Peter and Dona Miranda from England and hospital. What matters in life? Good health and that we are all here, together, with sincerity." The speech went on for a while longer, but he had never timed one of his unpredictable appearances better. Within a couple of hours all the furniture was upstairs and we could collapse. Yet again it did make us wonder why these significant moments seemed to be so definitely marked by a sense of crisis, and in a perverse kind of way it was encouraging.

8

"By setting forth the truth plainly we commend ourselves to every man's conscience in the sight of God." – Second letter to the Corinthians

It rained a lot over the next few days, and we discovered most of the places where the roof was leaking. Some others awaited the days when the wind was in another quarter. We learned to pick our way around the buckets and decided there was little point in bothering Zé Manuel until we had a complete list. Under these conditions it was no hardship to sacrifice field work for the winter atlas in order to go furniture hunting. This proved quite a challenge as most of the little money that the Trust still had in reserve was earmarked for finishing the improvements to the house. It was almost impossible to find second-hand furniture, as everything is of value in a country where resources are scarce, and so we hunted the shops of Portimão for bargains. In Senhor Fausto we found a kindred spirit.

His basement was crammed with baroque dressers of architectural magnificence, heaps of lurid lampshades stacked on flimsy metal garden chairs, and piles of mattresses. After his initial disappointment that we wouldn't contemplate buying one of the towering chandeliers that loomed over the dim corridors of the basement (the flat in Vila Verde had cured us for ever of any longings in that direction), he threw himself into the task of finding what we needed with great enthusiasm.

We set off on a tour of his family and acquaintances in different parts of the city in a search for beds and cupboards that would be cheaper than we could imagine. We found much of what we needed during that marathon day, and the rest over the next couple of weeks. Fausto got into the habit of turning up at Cruzinha with the latest finds in his van, some of which, like the oil paintings in violent orange, were not exactly our idea of essential equipment. We also grieved him by not accepting his pride and joy, a wardrobe beautifully constructed from Brazilian hardwoods, and we completely failed with our explanations about the disappearing rainforest. His wounded look said it clearly: As if the Brazilians don't have enough problems without people starting to be *esquisito* about their timber, and such a beautiful wardrobe too. But most of what appeared out of the van was exactly right, and before long the centre was sufficiently equipped to give a proper welcome to our first official resident visitors. For many, both Portuguese and *estrangeiros*, it was their first real contact with a Christian community.

We were convinced that most of those who found Christian belief a complete mystery, or irrelevant, had not rejected it, but simply had no idea of what it meant to believe in Jesus. The church (and of course very few people in Europe go to church anyway these days) often makes little sense because its worship and preaching, if any, is wrapped in a package of strange language and curiously sub-cultural behaviour. Outside the church it is rare to encounter any expression of the Christian life that isn't propaganda. John Stott has written: "Many people are rejecting our gospel, not because they conceive it to be false, but because they perceive it to be trivial. People are looking for an integrated world view that makes sense of all their experience. We learn from Paul that we cannot preach the gospel of Jesus without the doctrine of God, or the cross without the creation."

So we wanted Cruzinha to be a place where people with any or no beliefs could feel completely at home. All of us who worked on the team had a definite Christian commitment and on the basis of a shared concern for the natural world we wanted to provide a context for those who were staying to see what the Christian life could mean. I use the word "mean" advisedly, because in the very verbal culture of Europe, we are constantly exposed to a barrage of differing claims for a variety of different lifestyles, products, and solutions to our problems. Words and explanations can easily have a limited value, so it is one thing to hear what Christians say and quite another to see what they mean. In the way we worked and lived at Cruzinha we wanted to give the gospel human expression. We hoped of course that it would lead to discussion, but we didn't expect that it would necessarily be the most useful way to communicate what we meant. We hoped that by struggling tó apply the gospel in a practical way to the difficult problems of the environment we could spread its message more plainly than by adopting a more conventional approach.

One of our favourite places on the coast near Cruzinha is Ponta da Piedade. The sandstone cliffs are deeply eroded and there is often a heavy Atlantic swell crashing into the caves and around the stacks and islands at the point. Occasionally an incoming wave meets the backwash from the base of the cliffs, and peaks in a confusion of spray. Life at Cruzinha could feel

like that sometimes, because so many of our visitors came unannounced, including quite large groups of schoolchildren. If we were under pressure to finish reports, or looking after other visitors while dealing with one of the frequent difficulties with the water supply that arose in the early days, then it was hard to keep our nerve as the demands combined, and we often felt we had gone beyond our ability to respond.

Those times obviously posed a serious risk to any attempt to embody the gospel in the way we hoped, given that we were such flawed people. But it seemed to us that because we were rightly concerned to convince others of the life in Christ which we valued so highly, we needed to be even more careful not to confuse evangelism with propaganda. Evangelism is the work of every Christian and is the task of communicating the truth about Jesus. Propaganda is an edited and cleaned-up version of the truth, suitable for public consumption. The widespread use of propaganda leads to rapid disillusionment for those half-persuaded by what they have been told, and to unreality within the Christian community as people struggle to match up to the official version of what the Christian life looks like.

At Cruzinha we wanted to give an opportunity – painful for us at times – for Christians to be observed at close quarters where such dissimulation would be impossible. The communal life of a working field study centre means that visitors and staff see a great deal of each other at all times of the day and, if we are ringing waders or Storm Petrels, at night too. Projects do not always go according to plan, and often there is pressure if people are trying to work while getting to know another group of strangers. But it is only what Paul talks about when he says the apostles were made a spectacle. They were highly visible, in all their frailty, to everyone around. If it is true that as believers Christ is in us, then we had no reason to be worried that he would not vindicate his own presence. The contribution made by our failures and inadequate witness would not obscure him completely.

I remember one particularly torrid week when everyone was at far less than their best. It was probably the result of insufficient sleep with wader ringing and an unusually large number of unexpected visitors coming to the house, but there were some moments when things became quite tense. We faced the usual discrepancy between the peaceful pace of the visitors who were enjoying all they saw in the countryside around the house, and the endless demands on the team who were trying to keep everything running smoothly while doing fifty jobs at once. However, the letters from people who had been with us that week made it seem that they had spent their time in paradise. It did not stem from any careful window-dressing on our part, because most of the time we were incapable of putting on a front.

The core of the matter is Jesus's teaching that he is the way, the truth and the life. He is the way, and that means that for all our visitors, only in Jesus is there a path to God. Many of those who stay here are far more impressive and seem far more calm and coherent than we do, but it remains true. So we pray they may find him.

Among our early visitors were a couple with three small children, unmarried Vegans with an unswerving determination to live sensitively in the fragile environment of the planet. It is quite a challenge to encounter such radical commitment. Their serenity was impressive, not least because at the time we were trying to cope with a particularly full house. But the way they were choosing of quasi-Buddhist reverence was no path to God, although there were many things they could teach us. The way is Jesus, not us, and we are the signposts not the journey.

Jesus is the truth, and so that is our first point of reference. We have no obligation to any Christian package. We have no option but to be honest about him and ourselves. Any per-suasion must be on the basis of integrity and honesty, not wishful thinking or convenient half truths about our experi-ence of God or lack of it. I can think of many conversations with many people, and often they are in the form of an adven-ture, because genuine questions need genuine answers. By definition, if we are going to listen to each other, we do not know where the conversation will lead us. Our relationships with each other and those who stay can be taken at face value, and hold no hidden agenda. We have no responsibility to change anyone, which is God's business anyway, but simply to accept and to love them.

Jesus is the life, and relationship with God is about life, and not a separate activity called religion which is practised in separate places at separate times. If he is not as apparent in our field work as in our worship then we have not understood him.

After nine years in Portugal we still feel that this combination of an open and applied approach to the Christian life does in fact communicate the truth quite well. We have seen it making sense to enough people to persevere even if at times it is costly; there have been plenty of occasions when we have let God and each other down quite publicly. It is sometimes difficult to be faithful to the truth when the house is full of people who behave and live quite differently from Christians. Any group will spread out its own values for approval, and the pressure to conform to people's expectations can be great. If they think it is quaint to be Christian, you can feel quite quaint. I can think of one student group who stayed for a fortnight in the early days, and as we cleared out the piles of empty vodka bottles from their rooms at the end of their visit we remembered how when they arrived, they were faintly hostile, and so we felt vaguely bruised. But as we stayed true to what we were, instead of a group they became different individuals with various needs and uncertainties, and in the weeks following their departure a series of surreptitious thank-you notes arrived. We have seen that happen often enough now to be more confident, and less vulnerable, and perhaps it is better now that we have a larger team who can generate a more visible expression of faith, and give it a more varied form. But it seems to be true that no one confuses our imperfect expression of the Christian life with the reality of the gospel, and that Jesus does become apparent. How people wish to respond to that is of course their own affair, and if we were closer to godliness it would all work far better than it does – but it does work.

In practical terms our basic minimum of formal Christian

expression was to give thanks before eating, regardless of who was there. Depending on who was responsible for convening the meal, which could be difficult enough if it came to the table when everyone was busy with something else, then grace was in Portuguese, or English, sung or said. The acoustics of the narrow dining room proved to be as good as many a cathedral crypt, so we sang by preference. Those who wished to could join us for worship on Sunday mornings and evenings, always highly informal and as free of jargon as we could manage. During our worship, one of the team would read and explain a Bible passage that he had reached in his own Bible study, and we were often astonished at how relevant it was, and how clearly the writing spoke for itself. Admittedly, we had the advantage of living and working together, even if for some it was only for a few days, and when a local church gathers it is a much more disparate group. Nevertheless, the same remarkable relevance of a Bible passage to many of those present is often the experience of a good local church.

We were frequently surprised by who wanted to be there and who didn't, but no one was under any pressure. We met as a team to pray early one morning a week, although quite often the demands of the ringing programme during autumn migration played havoc with that. The rest of the time we endeavoured to pray for and support each other and everyone staying in the house.

What has also become obvious over the years as we have talked to many people at Cruzinha is that the way the church sometimes lives and works can produce far more casualties than we realise. We meet them all too often, and they make up what could be called a negative audit, but one that needs to be taken into account all the same.

We hear sometimes of successes and of growth, and there is much to learn from how it comes about, and much for which to give thanks to God. We have been greatly encouraged by churches to which we have belonged, in Europe and else-where, which have helped many people to faith in Christ, and which have grown fast. But we also need to listen to those who have battled with what they have encountered in the

church, and who feel their genuine difficulties have been dismissed. All of us who lead churches need to heed these misgivings.

Some of these doubts have been expressed by people who have been told they were failing through lack of faith when their early experience of God didn't match up to the version they had been given to expect. When they felt ill at ease with the way worship was conducted they were told it was lack of godliness. At one end of the scale we have friends in the village who cannot go to local churches, despite a genuine hunger for God, because they are too overwhelmed by emotions that they feel are artificially manufactured by those leading the services. Until recently there have been no alternatives. At the other end, friends in other churches find that worship is a tedious formality, devoid of a sense of God's presence, and far removed from their daily life. The challenge to those of us who lead worship is to find ways of expressing our love for God that stem from what we experience each day of the week. We need to find both an honest response to his love for the real world, and a gate to heaven.

It would occasionally happen that visiting Christians would begin almost to create a conspiracy to influence the others who were staying who would not call themselves believers. We would have no part in any of that. We care very much that everyone has the opportunity to believe in Jesus. But before anything else we are human beings created in the image of God, and belief does not divide us socially into a group in the know, or on the inside, and a group on the outside. Any concern on our part to share our faith is open to all, and not part of a secret process. Again this is basic Christian teaching. Paul writes to the Corinthians: "We have renounced secret and shameful ways, we do not use deception nor do we distort the word of God. On the contrary by setting forth the truth plainly we commend ourselves to every man's conscience in the sight of God." Perhaps it is a concern for results and the unconscious influence of dishonest sales techniques which have corrupted the relationships that Christians sometimes make with others, and of course we are fallible in this as in anything else.

We need to take seriously how destructive it can be. It is sobering to reflect that Islam had its birth in a reaction to a corrupt church, and that much of its hostility to Christianity in many countries of the Middle East still stems from the follies of the Crusades. So it needs to be stressed again that our friendship is offered at face value because we are human, and not for any other reason. What we do to make the gospel known, and how we try to do it, is open to all.

Of course we cannot ignore the fact that many of our visitors have difficulties with Christian belief per se. Sometimes they find what we believe unacceptable, and even when both they and we have had a chance for proper explanations, we must agree to differ. We have found that one essential Christian belief in particular is a constant irritant to many people; they cannot understand why Christians cannot agree that everyone's beliefs are equally valid and should be left unchallenged. Because we believe the gospel to be true, it follows that we hold alternative ideas about God (or no God) to be false, and seek to challenge them, albeit courteously and with integrity. This is often anathema. "You're entitled to your beliefs, but you shouldn't want to change mine," was how one student put it over lunch one day. "That is so arrogant."

This has meant that while nearly everything A Rocha does seem to meet with warm approval from everyone, at this point we are less popular. The fact that we have come to Portugal, and into the conservation world, not just with certain beliefs but with a message, is absolutely unacceptable. The very positive section about Cruzinha in the early editions of *The Rough Guide to Portugal* concluded regretfully, "There is a proselytising side to their work however . . ." The comment was later withdrawn, and other secular articles have not stumbled over our Christian identity, but the confusion between proselytising and mission is firmly rooted in the way that many people think. Even in churches there is a cluster of misunderstandings about concepts such as conversion and overseas mission, and sometimes we have had an uneasy reception when speaking about A Rocha, because we believe in both. Why we do, and what we believe, needs some explaining.

9

"The degrees and kinds and complexities of this showing forth of our inheritance must vary to an almost limitless extent." – David Jones

At a conference in Bangkok in late 1972/early 1973, some voices in the World Council of Churches called for a moratorium on international mission. The resulting discussion about whether the time of mission was past generated an unease in many churches about any work that went beyond famine relief or development projects. There was a feeling that national Christian organisations were now so well established everywhere, and that the risk of cultural imperialism was so great, that it would be preferable if people stayed in their own countries. Furthermore, an awareness of how far European culture has gone from any Christian roots meant that the real priority was seen as being at home. On the housing estates and in the tower blocks of our parish in Upton, there was a minimal Christian presence, and serious social problems. Not surprisingly we were often asked, "Why go off to Portugal if you really want to be missionaries? Isn't there enough to do around here? At least people in other countries are happy in their beliefs." But in all of this there are some truths and some real delusions.

Brian Stanley in *The Bible and The Flag* has made a clear case to show that early missionaries were not the simple accomplices of imperialism that they have often been accused of being. In many areas they recognised the identity and rights of local communities and did all they could to protect them against the ambition of colonial interests. While it is easy to find naive and damaging exceptions, it is generally true that where biblical mission has been accomplished the benefits have been great, both culturally and spiritually.

Nevertheless we now live in a new era where the initiative rests more and more with the newer churches of Latin America, Africa and Asia. The traditional sending churches find that frequently their material resources are not matched by their vitality, while the newer but under-resourced churches have a remarkable vision and life that is often lacking in Europe, North America, Australia and New Zealand, the former sending areas. Kwame Bediako, a Ghanaian Presbyterian, writes:

> The late twentieth century has seen a shift in Christianity's centre of gravity. The heartlands of the Christian faith have ceased to be the old Christendom of western Europe and are now to be found in Latin America, in parts of Asia and Oceania, and in Africa. It is not only in numerical strength that the Christian communities of the southern continents are more dominant on a world scale; they are becoming important also in ordering the Christian agenda on a world scale.

So the picture is of a worldwide international church that is variously strong and weak, but which has much both to give and to receive across the national boundaries. Raphael Akiri of Tanzania said of his time in Britain, "People have begun to realise that neither material prosperity nor poverty gives anybody automatic right to 'do' mission or to be 'missionized'. In my opinion the level of awareness about this is very low in Britain ... Giving [people or money] without being prepared to listen and receive is no longer acceptable." The task is to see who in the worldwide Christian community needs to contribute what, and who needs help. Tokunboh Adeyemo has written: "The task of world evangelisation demands a response from all of us – East, West, North and South. No single part can do it all alone. The North must come with its long heritage and contemporary resources; the West with its financial and technical expertise; the South must bring its people and passion for souls, and the East should not be left out."

The irony is that in fact it is often harder to receive than to give, particularly if you are used to being a giver not a receiver.

The convictions about mission that brought A Rocha into being were very simple, but also as relevant to the world as it now is as we could make them. We are still the inheritors of Jesus's clear command to the first disciples to spread the word around. Then as now, if the gospel was being frequently repeated in one area, and there was no one to explain in another, then it made sense to spread out. This is neither complicated nor a form of imperialism. The number of articulate and committed Christians in the south of Portugal is very few while on Merseyside they can be counted in thousands, so it made sense to go. In Bragança in the north of Portugal, a university teacher recently tried to form a Bible study group, but could not find one student among over a thousand in the college to help him. In 1991 the Grupo Bíblico Universitário estimated that in the country as a whole, out of a hundred and twenty thousand students there were around a hundred who were both capable of explaining the meaning of the gospel to their colleagues, and motivated to do so. In environmental issues worldwide, the number of Christians involved was tiny compared to those working in education, for example, so that too made strategic sense.

All this still applies to so many areas and is such an obvious truth that our immobility is astonishing. The conviction to stay where you are needs to be as strong as the conviction to go anywhere else, and needs to be formed in the light of the clear imperative to the whole church to preach the gospel. Mobility is built in to the description we are given of the early church, and is surely the meaning behind the lengthy descriptions of journeys in Acts. While it takes us only a few hours to travel distances that took many hazardous weeks for earlier missionaries, immobility is a dearly held tenet of contemporary British materialism, even to the point of ignoring the final journey that we will all make into the presence of God. It is occasionally implied that a good life insurance policy can prevent that departure too. There are still communities very nearby with no witness. These do not have to be geographically defined, they can also be recognised by social criteria, but they can be easily identified by anyone who cares about ensuring that these communities too have the opportunity to know about the God who loves them. The important thing is for the collective Christian community to think tactically and for the individual Christian to see life as necessarily at the service of mission.

This therefore begs the obvious question of what in fact mission is. Perhaps it has best been described in the recent goals of the Lausanne Congress as "using the whole church to bring the whole gospel to the whole world".

Perhaps, too, the inadequate pictures of the rich white church preaching to the poor dark world have been the cause of the widespread confusion that now prevails. Mission is the whole gospel because the gospel has never been just words about salvation. God did not send a voice from heaven or a letter, he sent Jesus. In his life was the message that we are cut off from God, and in his death and resurrection is the possibility of forgiveness, reconciliation and new life. In order for that message to have meaning or content to those who hear it, his disciples must live that life in the power of the Holy Spirit, and so mission will encompass the whole of human experience.

Christians who are involved in mission may be found doing practically anything that is biblical: transcribing languages into ASCII code, making television programmes, digging ditches, writing songs, caring for children, preaching and writing, counting cattle and waiting for hours in offices. Mission is not defined by any particular activity (although some, such as witnessing to Jesus, will be common to them all), but by the clear intention to live out what the Kingdom of God means. Therefore it does not necessarily involve crossing cultural boundaries, although because the possibility of the gospel being heard is often restricted within certain communities it frequently will.

It certainly means there is no professional class of missionary, supported by others who are not involved. Rather mission is the business of all Christians and will be the goal of their life whatever they do. There is no secular employment (or unemployment) for any Christian, there is only life in Christ, lived out according to our different callings. Whatever does not come from faith is sin, Paul says.

There will, however, always be international manifestations of mission, and the church itself needs the clarity of perspective that a cross-cultural exchange can bring. From the earliest days when Jesus talked to the Samaritan woman at the well the advantages for the clear understanding of the gospel became clear. As she cluttered Jesus's message with the Samaritan view of right worship, he firmly put it all to one side by stressing what was universally true. It is all too easy for one particular cultural clothing of the gospel to become the standard for all, and for one view to become the only one. It was obvious to the Jewish church that all believers should obey the Jewish law, because after all it was the Law, wasn't it? The problem was that to Gentiles it wasn't. The essential truth can easily become confused with the inessential trappings, and in the process dangerously changed. It is well known that western clothing has sometimes been seen as essential uniform for Christian communities in some parts of the world. Others have felt the need to cut off all contact with westerners in order to safeguard the true expression of their faith. Both extremes confuse the meaning of the gospel.

Sharing the work of mission with Christians from another culture gives an opportunity for a church to reassess what is essential, to see where it might have muddled the gospel with culture. When a Christian has to struggle with different cultural perceptions as he crosses a cultural boundary with the gospel, he has the opportunity to learn again what that gospel means in essence, and he can return to his own church with new insights, as Paul did to the Jewish church after seeing God unmistakably at work in Gentiles.

As British nationals in Portugal, we have not faced any significant struggle – unlike friends who have gone from Europe to Japan, or come to Britain from Africa. Not only have we stayed within Europe, but we have been here at a time when culturally Portugal has turned away from its historical orientation towards Africa, and drawn closer to the increasingly monolithic culture of its European neighbours. Even so, we are not at home.

The first time we invited friends from the village for supper, we had no idea that we had moved outside their limits of what was possible, and out of courtesy to clumsy foreigners they had no way of telling us, and so they accepted cheerfully. The food was ready by eight o'clock, but at nine thirty they still hadn't arrived and by ten we realised they weren't going to. We saw them the next day. "You didn't come," we said. "No," they replied, "we didn't," and there the matter rested.

We know now that of course they couldn't. They could not have considered going into the home of someone who was not family – no one ever does. Furthermore, by accepting hospitality they would have put themselves under an impossible obligation to return it, something they would never have felt confident about. In our village there are all kinds of reasons why it is not normal to welcome others into your home. Perhaps it stems from the suspicions engendered during the years of the dictatorship, but it also has to do with the need for privacy in a community where everyone is interested in everyone else.

These days we understand that the place to get to know people is in the street; but we have also discovered that, if our friends can bring the food, they love to come to our house, and don't feel under any obligation by doing so. If we are already under obligation to them for other reasons, they'll come cheerfully enough too. Jesus knew the value of being indebted to other people as his conversation with the Samaritan woman shows.

In Portugal, food is central to any social event, and in the summer friends come out from Portimão or down the lane from Vila Verde bringing their food to the charcoal grill under the rubber tree. We've had some wonderful occasions grilling sardines. Manuel really enjoys singing, and explaining just where we are going wrong with the things we have planted in the garden, and the women take over the kitchen.

All these perceptions of hospitality and home will undoubtedly shape the way that church life develops as Christ is slowly formed in our local friends. The important thing is that we leave the shaping to them.

The necessity of crossing cultural boundaries will also, we hope, stimulate us to be creative about the ways in which we take the gospel to others. One of the most challenging and disturbing books I have ever read about mission is Vincent Donovan's account of his work among the Masai, *Christianity Rediscovered*. At the outset he realises: "It was going to be a decidedly difficult task, bringing the Christian gospel of forgiveness, and the Christian understanding of salvation, to a culture so different from my own, a task calling for extreme care and delicate caution and much humility. So many mistakes could be made." As that gospel is clothed by a different culture, so new possibilities will emerge and he writes in the preface to the second edition:

> When the gospel reaches a people where they are, their response to that gospel is the church in a new place and the song they will sing is that new, unsung song, the melody that haunts all of us ... Two things must come together to lead us to that new place – the gospel and the sacred arena of people's lives. What we referred to tentatively in Africa as the naked gospel, what Karl Rahner describes theologically as the "final and fundamental substance of the Christian message" must be brought to bear on the real flesh and blood world in which we live ... "Preach the gospel to all creation," Christ said. Are we only now beginning to understand what he meant?

There had never been a bird observatory at the service of the gospel before, but why not? Come to that, why not a motorbike repair shop? The missing group in the church in much of Europe is the men (mostly, perhaps, because church activities tend to be so feminine in character – but that is another story), and if you want to be in contact with men, in our part of the world at least, you'll find them chatting in the motorbike repair shop. The mechanic is a kind of priest dispensing healing and wisdom in the area that really matters, that of the Zundapp and the Sachs. Why do missionaries (that unfortunate but apparently indispensable term) often seem to go to work only in the church while God is eager to work in the world too? How about a bistro in the south of France where there is a similarly minimal Christian presence? How about a theatre in Vienna, or a sports club in Madrid? In both places there are apparently few people able to explain what life in Christ means, and the churches which teach the Bible are tiny and would certainly appreciate a hand. Of course there are many innovative, compassionate and humbling projects already, but by establishing A Rocha we wanted to show that there are still plenty of unexplored possibilities for those concerned for mission in Europe.

In our case, conservation was our chosen field, and we had a few guiding ideas that encouraged us to feel that it would work well as mission, quite apart from the fact that it was a neglected area of Christian involvement.

First of all, conservation is by its very nature international. Many of those who read Rachel Carson's book, *Silent Spring*, in the 1960s were shocked above anything else by the revelation that toxic chemicals could be found in the tissues of plants and animals thousands of miles from their industrial source. The emissions from British chimneys destroy the forests and lakes of Scandinavia, and when Chernobyl burnt, radioactive rain fell thousands of miles away. Migratory birds do not respect national boundaries, and organisations that wish to protect them must be active across different cultures. This is home ground for the Christian because the gospel has been in the field since Pentecost.

It is tempting to speculate that one reason why Jesus carried out his ministry in Israel when he did was that a common language and the excellent communications of the Roman Empire could carry the message swiftly to many countries and cultures. The gospel was international and multi-cultural from the beginning. In passing, it is possible to see that sophisticated conservation organisations can sometimes make mistakes that the Christian church eschewed decades ago. Conservation has become international only very recently, and for the first time its protagonists face the challenge of communicating cross-culturally.

A recent article in a Portuguese conservation magazine explained how problematic that can be. The population of White Storks nesting in Europe has declined dramatically in recent years and so to find out more of the causes of the problem, many chicks were marked with colour rings while still in the nest. The idea was that when they returned from their African wintering quarters the following year, and could not easily be caught, a look at the rings on their legs could serve to identify the individual birds at a considerable distance. Unfortunately it was not appreciated that for many African children, a colour ring makes a fine ornament, and necklaces made up exclusively of colour rings have been seen in different villages. The birds became a prized target. The very scheme which was devised to help the birds in one continent was causing them to be hunted in another.

The modern church has battled throughout its history to interpret its message in different cultural contexts. Maybe Christians from both south and north who have a long experience of working internationally, and who are part of a kaleidoscopic worldwide family, can be of service here in sharing some of their hard-won lessons?

Secondly, conservation is by its very nature religious. As the World Wide Fund for Nature has come to recognise, people treat the world according to what they believe about it. In the Algarve, many of those who are altering the landscape so irreversibly see the world around them as nothing more than raw material for the money-making process, and act accordingly. Even the apparently natural features in the landscape are subject to the same belief; the Minister of Agriculture gave the game away recently by referring to eucalyptus plantations as "green petroleum". If the trees were grey or purple it could be no worse – the effect on the landscape is similar to laying asphalt, and the plantations exist to transform sun, rain and minerals into money via paper. They grow nearby on Monchique, and it is a sad experience to take a walk in the plantations. The trees stand above the bare earth around their roots, silent and still, harbouring no life. Nearby, it is still possible to find pockets of the vivid and complex woods of native oak and pine that they have supplanted, and to discover a whole community of insects and fungi among the profusion of different plants, and a wealth of animals and birds that live thereby. If you think the earth is there simply to enable us to get rich, then of course all that is of little interest, and the process of tearing up the woods to plant eucalyptus is logical.

The clearly religious element in all this makes it a very natural context for Christian involvement.

Finally we felt that a field centre would be an appropriate way of working in mission because we would constantly be with people. It goes without saying that however innovative the project, there is little point if it makes the gospel effectively unavailable. For different reasons the gospel in much of Europe has become locked within the ornate box of the church, and the rusting key dangles from the belt of religious professionals. In other places the key is in the lock, but the box is so ugly no one would guess the unutterable beauty and value of the contents. We were searching for a form that would do justice to the contents, and a field centre which could concern itself with what God had made in company with many people who were unsure that he even existed seemed a reasonable place to begin. That the search is extremely demanding is obvious. David Jones, the Roman Catholic artist and poet, suffered for a lifetime in the pursuit of what he called "valid signs". In the preface to his long poem *Anathemata* (which W. H. Auden called "Very probably the finest long poem written in English this century"), he writes of the acute difficulty within the present times of finding forms, an incarnation, for the thing itself, for what he wished to write. We did not therefore include among our hopes the thought that we would find an adequate expression for the thing we wanted to do, which was to give the gospel environmental expression. It was, however, worth a try.

Seeing field studies as a fruitful path for mission allowed us to challenge the commonly held idea that the way we keep body and soul together is in one box, and the Christian life is in another; in short, that mission is the prerogative of the religious enthusiast, preferably heroic to boot. But if a birder can be involved in mission, as a birder, then anyone can. If we restrict mission to certain types who are enthusiastic and heroic, we have travelled a long way from basic biblical thinking in two easy steps. If we leave mission to the religious, then inevitably it will become predictable.

Jesus shocked and surprised everybody all the time, but it

is rare for the church in Europe to surprise anyone. The range and creativity of his presentation of the gospel were astonishing. He commandeered boats, laid on food for thousands, drowned pigs, broke up funerals, wrecked temple furniture, wept and laughed. You could find him in a tête-à-tête with a prostitute, or surrounded by civic functionaries, on a mountain top, or walking across the lake. He ate and drank, fasted and prayed, was still, and highly mobile. He was silent and outspoken, could be found by lepers and beggars but lost by his parents. No one knew where he would turn up next. Quite honestly, where are we? If you ask anyone where we are to be found, if they know at all, they will tell you we are in church. If you ask them what we do, they will list religious activities. Where did they get that idea from? We gave it to them by making the gospel something for the church not the world, while Jesus's relationship with the religious was distinctly uneasy.

As the field studies at Cruzinha developed, we also gave

time to talking together about the ways in which they were formed by our life in Christ. It was necessary to make this a conscious exercise, because we found the instinct to compartmentalise went very deep in all of us. Only as time went on did it become less studied and more natural.

10

"For the ENGLISH TONGUE shall be the language of the WEST." –
Kit Smart

We had plenty of opportunity to earth some of these ideas as
the months passed. From early each day, as the shimmering
summer burned into a dusty autumn, the cicadas hissed in
the pine trees around the building and we battled with the
intricacies of a precarious water supply. By trial and error, we
began to discover how the routines of a residential centre in
the southern heat would develop in practice. Even so, one
obvious fact of life to which we would all have to adjust was
that routines would be scarce in a life which revolved around
a combination of the unpredictable movements of birds, and
the unexpected arrivals and departures of Portuguese students.
That was part of its charm, but it took some time to get everything organised. When it was rumoured by some visitors that
the cheese in the fridge had a sell-by date marked in Roman
numerals, we hoped it was merely malicious tittle-tattle.

   With the tempestuous advent of Dona Idalina, who offered
to come and help us clean the house a couple of mornings a
week, ancient provisions were no longer safe. Neither were the
belongings of the staff and visitors as clothes and equipment
disappeared into the vortex caused by her tornado style of
cleaning. To be fair to Dona Idalina, no other approach would
have shifted the piles of junk that accumulated in the dormi-
tories, but her impulsive reorganising has led at times to chaos.

One morning shortly after she arrived, I was working in the office when she came roaring in to clean. After some cursory swipes at the shelves with her duster, she reached over my shoulder, scooped up all the pens and pencils scattered over my desk, and plunged them decisively into my mug of coffee. Then, as always, I didn't have the nerve to protest, but we did draw the line when the computer was doused with water after she decided it would be a natural shelf for pot plants. Water has been the chosen medium for many of her more startling ideas, and she has fused the house several times by washing out the power points in the kitchen. On the final occasion, the bang was so loud that she was forced to agree it was better to keep them a little dirty. Like Miguel, whom we met at that time and who comes one day a week to help maintain the house and vehicles, she has become part of the family, and we would hate her to change her style. Each Christmas she writes an epic poem which describes her sense of grief at the misery in the world, and reads it during the lunch we have together, exhausting our supply of paper napkins.

Somehow, even without Dona Idalina's impulsive moments, the unpredictable continued to occur at Cruzinha with unnerving regularity. I will never forget the morning when Jeremy, who was eight at the time, was helping some workmen reconstruct a retaining wall at the boundary of our land. As they moved some of the fallen stones, he found some bones in the earth behind. His zoological instincts aroused, he collected them in a bucket, and brought them back up to the house to be admired and identified. I was showing a group of teachers around the newly finished education room when he appeared with his trophies and started to pass them round. I expected the usual collection of grasshoppers and snail shells and so I didn't pay much attention until I noticed one or two of the teachers looking a little quizzical, and saw that what he was showing them appeared to be part of a human skull. We've never pursued the matter since a local archaeologist confirmed that they were human bones, and even worse that they had only been in the earth for a relatively short time, in archaeological terms at least. We send out a Christmas letter with contributions from all the family giving the year's highlights, but were never really sure whether we should have allowed Jeremy's piece that year which began, with little regard for the festive season, "I found some bones in the wall – it was a dead lady."

We gave a priority to Portuguese visitors because we had come to work in that community. However, there were still relatively few people interested in any kind of field studies in Portugal, so it was clear that we would often have space for others. Similarly we discouraged Christian visitors who had no particular interest in the environment because a residential centre in the Algarve could easily degenerate into providing holidays and nothing more. We learnt that our hard-won language skills would often be unnecessary, as many of the students preferred to practise their English, and our children in particular, reluctant to practise their Portuguese, were only too happy to let them. We have found that the ideal picture of the bilingual family has not worked out in reality. Other families who live abroad have told us the same thing. They are often asked whether their children are completely fluent, as the myth dictates. Many aren't as it seems as though one language, usually the language the children are schooled in, will become dominant. English friends further north in Portugal have had difficulties in keeping their children's English going at all, and any questions they ask them in English get a Portuguese reply. We found the same in reverse, which is a real offence against missionary chic. The initial year they spent in the local *infantário* before going to the International School wasn't enough to make them truly bilingual even if it gave them a powerful local accent and many and varied ways of insulting their friends. The International School, despite its many virtues, did little for their Portuguese despite the fact that half the pupils came from local families, and so the children saw no point in struggling in Portuguese if they could make everyone else struggle in English. By the time we left Lagôa to move into Cruzinha, their informal tuition of Rui, our neighbours' son, was reaching quite an advanced stage, and the street echoed with his cries of "Jeremy, come 'ere, come 'ere."

The area of the estuary and farmlands proved to be as interesting all the year round as we had hoped, and slowly a pattern began to emerge in the activities of the house. We undertook a series of counts to discover the importance of the estuary for migrant birds, particularly for waders, and all the birds within the three square kilometres of the observatory study area were counted once a week. From the start there seemed to be a frightening amount of paperwork (an occupational hazard in all conservation jobs, I discover) and so I really appreciated the three-hour walk round a fixed route, recording all I heard or saw. Visitors contributed their own observations, and we rapidly built up a picture of what we might expect to see. Each time of the year had its own highlights, from the Black-tailed Godwits that came tumbling out of the sky in January to pause briefly on the marsh as they made their way north, to the precision arrival of the Bee-eaters on or around April 5th. Soon afterwards the nights were punctuated with the odd repetitive calling of Red-necked Nightjars, while during the day the vivid summer birds, Golden Orioles, Hoopoes and Woodchat Shrikes, brightened the green of the fig and almond orchards. They held our attention until the astonishing waves of migrants passed through the Algarve in protracted autumn movements which lasted from late July to mid-November. There were days when all the bushes seemed alive with Blackcaps, and Chiffchaffs flicked ahead of us from every tree as we walked the lanes. Even the onset of the first light frosts in December merely added to the movements of birds like Lapwings and Golden Plovers which arrived on our fields, escaping the rigours of the northern winter.

With the winter atlas completed, Mark undertook a detailed study of the small population of Black-winged Stilts on the marsh. Sometimes our visitors were able to compile reports from different fields, and we had geologists, botanists and entomologists both amateur and professional staying. Bob Pullan was able to combine his work at the University of Liverpool with field work in the area and produced a survey of the present and past status of wetlands in the Western Algarve, as well as bringing groups of students from the

university to use the centre. The ringing programme developed its own rhythm and we learned that the orange groves were important roost sites for many of the wintering finches and warblers. Among the enormous arrivals of wintering birds in early November were occasional rarities such as Yellow-browed Warblers and Richard's Pipits which helped to keep us going as we stumbled out into the freezing night to open the nets before dawn.

As planned, the ringing programme was an important activity from the first. For much of the year the weather conditions in the Algarve are reasonably predictable. It was possible to plan to spend a night on the marsh catching and ringing waders, or days out in the orchards ringing migrant warblers, without the risk of bad weather making the whole enterprise an endurance test for the visitors. On occasions whole families joined us and we found that the only birds many local schoolchildren had ever seen at close quarters had been hanging off their fathers' belts when they returned home from hunting. (Hunting comes in for a lot of criticism from British visitors to Portugal, but it has to be said that British cats kill at least as many birds as Portuguese hunters.) As we showed the children Blackcaps from Germany, or Swallows from Africa, we talked about the incredible complexity of the birds' plumage, and were able to show how each species was adapted for its life, how its wing shape suited the way it had to find its food, and the enormous journeys that they all undertook to find their way to the Algarve. For many people on the wader nights, used to living in towns and cities, it was the first time they had ever really looked at the night sky, or realised that birds were flying and feeding at night. To be in a small group, gathered round a gas lamp and reading the ring numbers of a bird from Finland, or seeing another that was heading for Senegal, made a deep impression and provided a direct meeting with the intricate design of the Creator.

In the evenings following days out in the field we ate together round the long wooden table, an antique extravagance from the north of Portugal that proved irresistible when we saw it for sale in Portimão. We reasoned that the chestnut tree from which it came had been felled so long ago that we could overcome our scruples. I think the Trustees have just about forgiven us.

Our local team was complete when Violinda volunteered to come down from Vila Verde each evening to make supper. She is built on a grand scale as if to prove beyond all doubt the virtue of her work, and as the *Rough Guide to Mediterranean Wildlife* wrote, "the traditional food at Cruzinha is outstanding". Her husband Délio is certain that she was the single cause for the frequent failure of the shock-absorbers on the long-suffering Red Rose as we clattered up the rough track back to her home in the village at the end of the evening. We paid the village mechanic (another Manuel) very cheerfully, because we and successive visitors have come to love Violinda dearly, and cannot imagine Cruzinha without her. On a recent April 1st (known here as *Dia de Mentiras,* Lies Day) she tendered a mock resignation and is still laughing at the panic it caused.

The meals were often memorable for all kinds of reasons. Eating in Portugal means time to talk, and the discussion often turned to the question of what was distinctively Christian about the environmental work of A Rocha. Occasionally we had Christian visitors in the house. They were usually enthusiastic about all they had seen in the countryside around the estuary, and had enjoyed being with the staff and accompanying the ringing or the botanical surveys. "So," they would say, "tell us about the Christian side of your work." The frequency of the question demonstrated that sometimes we were talking across a theological divide even though we may have shared identical views about Christian belief in general, and the authority of the Bible in particular. We tried to explain that we saw no distinction between the ringing and the other field work, and the Bible studies in the village, or times when we could talk about Jesus with students who were staying in the house. The former were not secular, and the latter were not spiritual. All were undertaken out of worship and obedience, and all mattered to the Creator and Redeemer of the world. Obviously the field work of an ornithologist who has no Christian commitment is indifferent to the Creator, but so is his church-going. Activities themselves are not divided into secular or spiritual categories, as Jesus made clear. "You diligently study the Scriptures because you think that by them you possess eternal life" (John 5:39). If there is nothing intrinsically spiritual about Bible study, then there is nothing necessarily secular about field studies. What then was happening in our field work, undertaken as a way of serving God and advancing his Kingdom?

First of all, it was worship. A definition of worship that sees it simply in terms of songs or hymns or conscious prayer does justice to one part only of the Bible's broader description. To return to Romans again, Paul says: "Offer your bodies as living sacrifices, holy and pleasing to God, this is your spiritual act of worship." (In passing, notice the effortless way he avoids the trap into which the church has repeatedly stumbled of making that which is material "unspiritual". The failure to value the physical world as God does, stemming from the

117

influence of Greek philosophy on early Christian thinkers, has been often cited as one cause of our indifference to the world around us.) As well as conscious and loving adoration, worship is seen as a direction of life in which we offer all that we are and do to the creator, looking for his glory. Significantly Jesus tells the rebellious Bible students in John's gospel that what they refuse to ask him for is life. As we mapped the last remaining sites of rare dune plants, or recorded the periods in which different migrants appeared in the observatory study area, we were taking notice of what God had made, coming to understand it in all its complexity, and consciously giving him the glory. Field work which strives to understand God's creation is true worship, and as such it can have an important bearing on our lives. If we do not understand the world around us, the way we live will almost inevitably be destructive of its delicate equilibrium.

When a golf course (another golf course . . .) was planned locally, there was, of course, an urgent need for water to irrigate it in a climate that is highly unsuitable for large areas of green turf. The simple solution was to dam the river, which was quickly and cheaply done. (It is amazing how powerful technology has erased the space for reflection enjoyed by previous generations.) Once the river was dammed, the estuary began to silt up to the point where the local community of fishermen could no longer reach the sea with their boats. At the time of writing a futile but immensely costly attempt to dredge the estuary is in process, and already it is clear that another set of unforeseen consequences is appearing. It goes without saying that any ecological implications which take even longer to discover, such as the impact on fish stocks or the loss of habitat for migratory birds, have received little attention. What is striking is the complete lack of humility which we demonstrate as we alter the environment in profound ways, with little or no understanding of the effects of our actions. While the introduction of Environmental Impact Assessments in Europe is a welcome departure, it is still all too easy for a developer to buy one off the shelf that is exactly suited to what he wishes to do.

So, understanding is an essential prerequisite for our inevitable transformation of the world around us, and humility a vital ingredient in the search for understanding. If we recognise that the world exists primarily for the Creator, and only secondarily to satisfy our material needs, we have a basis for that humility, and our active relationship with the Creator provides the context for the Christian field worker. In Genesis 9 we witness an agreement with God and his creation that is made specifically with people. It continues, however, to establish a direct relationship between God and his creation without reference to us. "This is the covenant I have established between me, and all life on earth," says God, with no hint of people as mediating in that covenant. Later in the Old Testament we read that Job was asked, "Where were you when I laid the earth's foundation?" We are at times a spectator in the vital relationship between God and his creation, and conscious of that, our work becomes worship. In giving others the opportunity to become aware of that dimension, our work goes on beyond worship to become witness.

It is witness, because the world was created to show out the character of God, to make it plain:

> The world is charged with the grandeur of God.
> It will flame out, like shining from shook foil;

wrote Gerard Manley Hopkins at the beginning of the poem from which this book derives its title. We have heard the same discovery from many people who have had little time or opportunity to watch the world around them carefully. The exclamations of the small group from an inner London school who joined us on the marsh just as the sun came up over the pines may have been in a different idiom, but they were talking about the same thing. The world can be an eloquent place.

It is one of the tragic results of urban design or lack of it worldwide that this God-given voice is so far removed from the hearing of most of the world's population. In many cities every object, every noise, every sight, speaks of humanity and our various follies and shortcomings, and the only witness of the created world comes from the dimmed flame which is the image of God in us all, and the square of sky above our heads. This places a heavy burden on the witness of the soloists, the redeemed world of God's people, in the absence of the orchestra, the creation. No wonder the tune sounds reedy at times, and seems almost to be drowned out by the noise of the machine.

We are aware of the immense privilege we have of a full orchestra as an Algarve sunset blazes over the hills to the west, or as a tiny warbler from Siberia finds its way to the olive groves behind the house. As life for millions of people is reduced to a struggle for survival, we know it is hardly a normal context for the words of the gospel. Nevertheless it is one of those that God intends, and one reason that wherever possible we involve visitors in our field work. It can mean counting Egrets back into the roost on the nearby cliff-stacks, or hauling poles down to the ringing sites, but we look for all the ways of bringing people in that we can find. I know from my own stumbling start in ornithology that it is all too easy for the expert staff of an observatory to make beginners feel that they are surplus to requirements, and so we work hard to give a genuine welcome to everyone who joins us in the field. It may not be a watertight logical proof of the existence of God to hold in your hand a Chiffchaff which has found its way back from Scandinavia to our orange orchard for the fifth year running, but we have seen that for many people it is a message of his care, not least when the team at Cruzinha are conscious that such events are the work of the Creator. Since Colin Jackson arrived from Kenya to join the team, these moments are marked by great shouts of "Glory!" Others show their delight more calmly, but there is a wide vocabulary of wonder.

Lastly, our field work is carried out in obedience to God. This is manifest at different levels. John Stott has always defended his passion for bird-watching by a light-hearted reminder that the verb Jesus uses when he says "Study the birds of the air" is an imperative. More seriously, however, the commission to be stewards of creation implies study, for the reasons given above.

Protection without careful study is of little value. Not far from Cruzinha was the only known colony of Purple Gallinules in Portugal. There was considerable concern for their future, and it was decided to prevent any disturbance of their habitat. Among those thereby excluded from the site was the local herd of cattle which used to visit the reedbed for lunch from time to time. Within two years bushes and trees were invading the reedbed, their new shoots reprieved from the attentions of the hungry cows, and soon afterwards the area dried up, neatly removing most of the Gallinules' habitat. Protection without understanding is hopeless.

Furthermore, obedience does not necessarily imply pain. It may well be that God asks us to deny our natural gifts and inclinations in favour of other work which we take up in obedience. Christian biography is full of examples of brilliant pianists who never touched the keys again, or sportsmen who never did anything more strenuous than carpet bowls after receiving a call to the Arctic. I was brought up in Christian youth groups on the stories of such renunciations, and of course recognised the central message that nothing matters more than to obey God, whatever the cost. Nevertheless it would have been good to have heard more of the natural gifts of those such as Wycliffe and Henry Martyn, both brilliant linguists, or Ruth Watson who had always loved mountains and so felt herself completely at home as a doctor in Nepal, and who offered it all to the service of the kingdom of God. Although God affirms what he has created as well as what he has redeemed, we often find it easier to recognise his activity in the abnormal and supernatural than in the normal and natural. Our experience in A Rocha has been that we are drawn together as a community of people with a deep feeling for the natural world and a passionate concern for its protection. It comes from different roots, and in many cases we would be hard pressed to articulate its causes, but the challenge has been to find its meaning within the worship and the work of God's kingdom.

For some of us, and for some of those who have supported A Rocha, there has been a problem with this, because the

Christian agenda undoubtedly has more pressing business. I remember returning to the UK to speak about A Rocha the day after the Armenian earthquake. It was hard to talk about disappearing habitats and environmental degradation in the context of such terrible human suffering. Another year I arrived in England to find that the church was preoccupied by the dangers of New Age teaching, and I met several people who were convinced that any Christian working with environmental issues must necessarily be following a New Age path towards heresy. There will always be urgent concerns, but it is a poor organisation that never attends to the smaller items on its agenda. Appalling needs in other areas do not imply that there is no place for work in the environment. In fact, as Rowland Moss explains clearly in *The Earth in Our Hands*, it isn't possible to separate human and environmental needs: "The point is that environmental problems and man's abuse of God's world are inextricably linked with the rich–poor polarity apparent in the world economy." But it was also Rowland Moss who pointed out that it is Christians with their understanding of the value of the natural world to God, who have a powerful reason for working to protect the environment even when it is not clear that any human benefit can be derived from what they do.

The wide biblical canvas similarly gives us reason to follow a calling to a detailed corner far removed from the desperate events that may well occupy the centre of the picture. However, the fact of the incarnation in an obscure town should warn us away from precipitate judgments about where precisely the centre of the picture is located. At times Christian organisations seem to make claims for the importance of their work based upon criteria which reflect the preoccupations of the secular news agencies, but perhaps we should all be cautious about defining God's agenda too carefully beyond what we find his concerns to be in scripture. Certainly the care of the earth has its place among those concerns, and it will remain important even if it should become unfashionable in the media as rapidly as it became fashionable. It will never be easy for individuals to live responsibly in societies which are reluctant to make the sweeping structural changes necessary to halt the rapid degradation of the planet, but there is a growing volume of information and advice from Christians and others about what practical steps we can take.

We have not found it easy to live consistently with our conviction that it is important to respect the creation by the way we live. In order to run the house at all we soon had to buy a minibus to join the Red Rose, and those who come from the north of Europe tend to arrive by plane. Although as a family we have felt so uneasy with the way meat is produced that we have adopted a limited degree of vegetarianism, it is so far removed from current Portuguese practice that we haven't felt we could impose it on the centre menu. We compost all our vegetable waste, but in the dry Mediterranean climate it doesn't rot down well unless you keep it moist by watering in the summer and thereby use another precious resource. Until recently we have been unable to get recycled paper, but we have now got a few bottle banks in the area. We have one or two practical projects on the go most of the time. Some, such as worm-farming, haven't worked out, but others, such as replacing all the exotic trees around the house with native hardwoods, and learning how to propagate some of the more common scrub species, are going well.

Until recently recycling was second nature to everyone around here, and often if you didn't bring a plastic bag to the shop you'd have to take things home in your pockets, or buy one in the market, because you'd never be given a new one. Bread was always fetched from the bakers in a cloth bag. Bottles were far too precious to be thrown away. The deposit system was so ramified that we never fully unravelled it but often you couldn't take a bottle out of a shop unless you brought an empty in with you. How you were ever supposed to break into the system in the first place remained a mystery. To those who had more was given, and that was an end to it. Travelling was usually environmentally friendly because any car going anywhere was as crammed with passengers as a Kenyan *matatu*. When we first arrived in the country, Tom Wilson had fitted the five of us, Alison, and all our luggage for a year into his Renault 4, stacking children between the cases and the roof like an experienced storeman.

Much of this has changed now and we are as wasteful a society as any other in Europe, which is widely regarded as a sign of progress. Our friends drive in alone to work, and the faded vegetables in the hypermarket are embedded in yards of cellophane and expanded polystyrene. They'll give you twenty plastic bags to put it all in if you want. Wide new roads from nowhere to nowhere are scarring the landscape, and the old agriculture of almonds, olives, figs and carobs which used no water and had no pests is replaced, if at all, by thirsty citrus groves needing regular doses of insecticide to survive, and threatened by epidemic disease at any moment. It's hard to be responsible in the way you live, but we know there is no option but to continue to work at it.

Living at Cruzinha, in a little corner of Europe without a television, we run the risk of becoming insular and out of touch. However, we are also more able, perhaps, to observe how rapidly the church can shift in its focus of interest, how in Britain it is the television which often seems to set the agenda for discussion, and how nine-hour journalistic wonders leave little permanent mark on the real shape of Christian involvement in society. We return to Britain only every couple of years which serves to foreshorten the wave-lengths of fashion which ripple through the country and the church. It is hard to adjust, and on arrival we are always afraid of seeming quaintly irrelevant. Nevertheless perhaps this opportunity to be an outsider is also a bonus for those involved in mission. The inconvenient and odd perspectives of some-one from overseas can be a resource for a community willing to examine its assumptions in the light of those from another culture. As the British church increasingly needs and wel-comes the contribution of people from other Christian com-munities around the world it will have to struggle to accept their commentary, as in the past other cultures have often struggled with the British view of things.

The title of a Christian student magazine in Cambridge in the early 1970s was *Really?* and it reflected its wry challenge

to believing and unbelieving students. The title was a good one, because it implied that some listening had been done first, but there is always a place for questioning how important some of the current concerns really are. Because a wide range of visitors come to A Rocha from many different countries, and with many different beliefs, we have to subject our convictions about the importance and direction of the work we are doing to that kind of scrutiny, and it hasn't always been easy. While Dona Dora was here she imported boxes and boxes of used clothes for distribution in the area. She felt strongly that we should open a rehabilitation programme for local disabled people. Frank had ideas for a nursery that would supply native plants to landscape gardeners. Dave Okill was appalled at how little time we gave to mapping the distribution of rare birds of prey, and ringing the chicks. While some visitors never understood why we should do any ringing at all, others failed to see why we should close down the ringing programme on Sundays.

After all the discussion over supper, the evening would end in the common room talking, or reading, or watching interminable slides if some of the Lisbon students were down for the weekend and had brought their latest pictures of unidentifiable gulls on the horizon. As winter came round again we had a wood fire, burning scrap timber from the building sites of Portimão so as not to contribute to the deforestation taking place throughout the Alentejo, where oak woods are being cut down to heat the villas of the Algarve. And so with the onset of tremendous thunderstorms and torrential rain we came to the end of the first full year of work at Cruzinha.

11

"For the right names of flowers are yet in heaven." – Kit Smart

Early the following year, we became aware for the first time of something that was often to prove our biggest challenge to faith. It was impossible to stop the clock and hold on to everyone who had come to be part of the team, and who then felt like one of the family. I remember that in the earliest discussions about the house there was some disagreement about whether or not those who worked here would be known as the staff. In fact they often are, but it has never felt like Us and Them. In practice it feels more like an extended family, and so when anyone leaves it is like a little bereavement.

Mark had come on a three-year contract, and now had the offer of a PhD on gulls which would be a good entry into academic ornithology. For us it was our first hard lesson in letting go. We've subsequently moved into the post-graduate levels as the children have gone off to boarding school. You never get used to it, and even as I write we are endeavouring to come to terms with life without Colin whose irrepressible personality has filled the house for the last three years. Next year it will be time to imagine how we can manage without Will's quiet wisdom and kindness.

More than that, we have discovered that people always seem irreplaceable. We all knew that we wanted Cruzinha to be run by a Portuguese team, but there were very few active Christian students, and of those we met even fewer had any great interest in the environment. So for the time being we needed to find people from outside the country. It was hard to imagine Cruzinha without Mark because he had always been so totally committed to A Rocha, and his gifts were ideally suited to all that the project was trying to do. But an important part of A Rocha's work was to equip people with a biblical context for their working life in conservation or environmental studies once they left, so there was nothing for it but to let Mark go.

Typically his time with A Rocha ended with one of those bizarre illnesses that seemed to be a feature of those years. He contracted reactive arthritis, possibly from a tick bite, and for over a year suffered great weakness and could walk only with difficulty. Medical improbabilities were becoming all too familiar, but even so they were not without their funny moments. Frank, Maria and Manuel's beloved Franco, had also come to grief, but this time on a motorbike in Pakistan while travelling to a refugee camp. When he and Mark met in England they were both bandaged and hobbling around on crutches. We began to wonder if work at A Rocha should carry a government health warning.

None of this seemed to deter Sarah Neden from coming to join us as Mark left. We wanted to broaden our work to include a closer study of the habitats of the western Algarve, and Sarah's particular interest was botany. She had the unenviable task of putting plant studies on to the agenda of a place dominated by birders, but she managed to lay a foundation that others were able to build on. Many of our visitors, particularly in spring, were at least as interested in plants as birds, and all that Mark and I had been able to offer was a kind of "Bluffers Guide to the Geranium": "Blue, was it? Plumage a little ragged? Probably one of the Geraniums I should think."

It was a great relief to be able to give some genuine information about the profusion of wild flowers and plants in the fields around the house: orchids and field gladioli, narcissi and irises. Suddenly we all became more aware of this new world at our feet. Sarah's other great gift was marshalling the volunteer wardens who started to arrive in numbers once word of A Rocha began to spread in student circles.

I think we have now experienced every kind of volunteer. Some, like Colin, and Will Simonson who is a botanist of rare ability, have immediately fitted in so well that they have subsequently joined us on the full-time team. Others have been here for only three weeks, but it has seemed a lot longer, no doubt to them as much as to us. We have had nurses chopping firewood, and a psychiatrist painting the book-shelves. Mostly they have been students, but we have also had doctors, actors, a plumber, farmers, musicians, photographers, ornithologists and, at the time of writing, our second retired policeman. The slang that inevitably develops has categorised them into vol wols, hol wols, and finally, using the Portuguese word for sun, sol wols.

Epitomising this last group was a student – we will call him George – who appears in all the photos in a meditative pose as he watches everyone else digging out some pools we were making for amphibians. He was transferred on to the less strenuous decorating team, but finally the heat proved too much for him, and he disappeared off to the beach, leaving as a sign of his departure an open twenty-five-litre can of paint, value fifty pounds, to dry in the sun.

Others, the true vol wols, we remember as much for the wonderful food they produced as for the work they did. Thanassis bought a sheep from the shepherd who is our neighbour, and roasted it whole in true Greek fashion over a wood fire one night for an appreciative houseful of thirty-two Portuguese students undeterred by a violent thunderstorm that broke an hour before the meat was ready. The complicated structure of umbrellas, plastic sheets and bamboos stolen from the ringing equipment threatened to collapse more than once, but it was all worth it when the food was ready. One summer we were even blessed by a trainee chef who was keen to work for a Christian organisation overseas. I will never know how we managed to get to the head of that particular queue, but Stephen's speciality of Ulster Fry transformed a series of cold mornings on the marsh after nights spent wader ringing. For someone from such an upright protestant background he had a truly decadent repertoire of desserts, and in Colin he found the appreciative audience that a chef yearns for. By the time he left, chocolate meringues were being produced in industrial quantities, and meal appeared to follow meal in seamless succession.

The other gastronomic prize went to Bill and Liz Barge from Arkansas. They had apparently found retirement in Arkansas a little dull, and for some years had been travelling through Europe with a small handgrip in which were their overalls and a few other essentials, offering their skills in carpentry, cooking, and anything else anyone needed, to Christian projects. Several of their six children worked in refugee camps in South America, so they went there too from time to time, but they were able to spend a month with us. So it was that we were introduced to corn bread and ways of cooking chicken that Violinda had never thought of, and a series of Deep South expressions entered the house vocabulary, "F'r g'dn'ss sakes". We had already discovered that the Mennonites were one of the few churches to be serious about environmental problems, and Bill and Liz gave us further reasons for a deep respect for all things Mennonite. A series of fine display panels and varnished kitchen cupboards still bear witness to their skills.

The only volunteer noted for his disregard of food was Mike the Bike, and it was less a lack of appetite than a preference for long-distance sleeping. The latest of early starts to open the nets was enough to render him catatonic for days. The problem first emerged on a night ringing waders. "Are you managing okay, Mike?" Colin asked him. "Yes, I'm fine, I just keep falling over." Several times at supper he laid his head down by the soup plate, and was well gone by the time the next course arrived. The only thing that could be guaranteed to galvanise him into action was an excuse to go somewhere on Mark's motorbike, which even before Mike took to using it was looking a little the worse for wear. If the ringers had forgotten a flask of coffee, Mike would go burning off round the dyke, his progress marked by a cloud of dust, and all too frequently interrupted by the echo of a distant thud as he misjudged a corner. We took to writing a checklist before leaving for the marsh in the interests of public safety.

In the early days the priority was to get the house workable, and to establish some simple environmental projects in the acre of land around the building. We wanted to produce some of our own fruit and vegetables, and so that meant planting and watering. There was work for any number of volunteers, and we were still at the stage of agreeing to every request. So when the phone went one morning and Fernando Cunha from the local Baptist church asked if Armando and Luis who were recuperating from heroin addiction could come for a month, we were happy enough to agree. "They just need a change of scene – they've had a few little problems, but they're okay really," he assured us. I count myself among the world's optimists, but as Fernando can make anyone seem like Ibsen with toothache we were not too surprised when we found that among the little problems were numbered armed robbery and

131

attempted murder. Despite these revelations their stay was reasonably uneventful, although it was perhaps a mistake to leave it up to them to lay out a small orange orchard. Some of the rows turned out decidedly wobbly and Manuel grumbles about it every time he comes down from the village to inspect the trees. The money and equipment they took when they left was removed peacefully and later returned.

Everyone who came had to pitch in with whatever was going on at the time. We put in small pools and a couple of hides, and cut down some of the eucalyptus trees we had inherited, replacing them with native species like cork oaks and carobs. There were rides to cut for the ringing nets, and educational displays to prepare for the big room Zé Manuel had added to the house. Mark's talent for drawing was much in demand as we prepared some panels for local schoolchildren which taught them how to identify birds, and what species to look for in the different habitats. There were a few nervous moments with one display which lit up if a drawing of a bird was correctly linked to its name. Until Colin, then on his first

132

visit as a volunteer, made the wiring completely safe, there was always a risk that it would light up the eager child as well.

We had to get used to the idea that the number of visitors was growing fast, and so paths and signs needed making. Slowly the area began to look more cared for, and we were able to give more time to field work and to the beginnings of the campaign to protect the area from development. The most effective way to begin was to enthuse as many people as we could about the beauty and value of what we were learning about the Alvor. Conservationists often complain that the only time the environment ever receives any attention in the press is when a disaster has occurred. If a tanker runs aground, or a forest dies, the environment is invoked. It is harder to find any more positive references. So we started by going to all the local primary schools with a talk and some slides about what the children could find in the countryside around. At the time a beautifully illustrated bird book was available to give to the children, and so the visits were always a great success. In turn, some of the schools brought their children to Cruzinha.

At the other end of the educational ladder, we wrote up all the studies in Observatory Reports, and distributed them as widely as possible. We aimed to produce them as rapidly as the other European observatories, and for their content to be similarly professional. Because we were known as a Christian organisation, it was all the more important to produce work of the highest possible standard. The biggest headache was always translating the finished work so that it was available in both English and Portuguese. Eventually we took to inviting all the students who had come during the year, and whose English was good enough, for a weekend in February, and we attacked the piles of paper together. It worked reasonably well for a couple of years, but then was the victim of its own success; everyone enjoyed it far too much to achieve a great deal, and the students returned to Lisbon to recover from lost sleep, the texts untouched in their rucksacks.

The supremo of these occasions was the inimitable Gonçalo

who first appeared at Cruzinha as a second-year student. Polymath, a brilliant pianist and amateur astronomer, he also had the names of all the birds on the European list in his head in most of the major world languages, and was working on some in Chinese. If provoked he would chant them unstoppably which we found could induce a strange vertigo at the end of a tiring day. During the wader nights we used to limit him to twenty-five questions an hour in order to preserve our sanity, but without his remarkable energy many of our reports would never have seen the light of day. His translations were meticulous as well as lightning fast, and when we were finally able to acquire a computer and tackle the logging of all the data that had accumulated, his keyboard skills made him far faster than any of us. He preferred to work into the small hours with classical music playing loudly, but it was a small price to pay. Perhaps even more importantly, on each of his visits from Lisbon (he was another one who preferred to travel at night – I have sometimes wondered if this all goes back to the Arab desert journeys) he brought different students whom he was introducing to the delights of birding à la Gonçalo, a high-energy business involving a lot of gesticulation and exclamation and plenty of glimpses of the birds fleeing from the uproar. Those who survived the experience returned often, but none of them as regularly as Gonçalo who came over a dozen times each year. Now he is a graduate he has calmed down a lot, although he continues to take on work at a remarkable rate.

Apart from the slide presentation and occasional visiting groups of children, a thoroughgoing schools programme had to wait until such time as we could find team members from within Portugal with the needed gifts and enthusiasm. There were never enough hours in the day for the work that was already underway. Furthermore, as the months passed and we learned more about the local environment, it was not always possible to do as we had hoped and to adopt a completely positive approach to all that was happening, by giving most of our time to informing and enthusing children and their teachers. Each week seemed to bring another threat to the best habitats around us, and we found it hard to stand by and watch.

12

"Let Shuni rejoice with the Gull, who is happy in not being good for food." – Kit Smart

"We'll need more water by the weekend," Miranda said one morning. "Why don't we make a quick dash up to Monchique to fill up the bottles?" We collected all our drinking water that way, usually making a trip every few weeks. A few hours later we stood on top of the hills and looked down at the estuary, unable to believe our eyes. A pall of smoke rose from the marsh down by the coast, and already it was drifting some miles back towards where we stood. The land that was burning was one of the last remaining examples of saltmarsh vegetation for miles around. Apart from rare plants and reptiles, the area held Bluethroats and Jack Snipe in winter, while Black-winged Stilts and Yellow Wagtails nested in summer, all species that are becoming rapidly more uncommon in Europe as wetlands everywhere are drained.

As quickly as we could, we finished filling the bottles and went back down to Cruzinha to discover the extent of the damage. Much of the marsh was charred and smoking, the vegetation burnt in the vain hope of providing some rough grazing for cattle. When the first small fires had been started some days before, we had tried to talk to the people concerned, but the land was rented out, and neither owner nor tenant was particularly interested. "It's just waste ground – there's plenty of that around," was all they said. They had not

explained that nearly half the marsh would be burnt by the time they had finished.

When we first moved here, it took some time to appreciate the vivid, sometimes harsh, beauty of the Algarve. We were more accustomed to the pastel colours and soft contours of West Wales, and had to learn to understand the feel of the different seasons, and the more extreme character of the local environment. As time passed, we came to admire the remarkable ways that plants and birds had adapted to conditions that were quite demanding at different times of the year, and there was great joy in exploring their intricately designed survival. The down side of that was the real distress that we often felt at witnessing their destruction.

Although we had chosen to site the A Rocha centre in a threatened area, and had felt the need to apply a Christian approach to real, rather than theoretical, conflicts of interest, sometimes the problems seemed to be coming too close to home. We had always known that an idealised project would be of little use, but the practicalities of frequent destruction were sometimes hard to bear. However, this is the context for many individual Christians working in secular conservation organisations, and as they face many tricky and unsatisfactory decisions each day, so we could ask for little else.

Bob Pullan's work had shown that over half of the local wetlands had been lost in the last thirty years, and the Alvor estuary was the last significant wetland to remain reasonably unaltered in the western Algarve. Around the shores of the estuary the patchwork of farmland and scrub had retained much of its original character, although the increasing abandonment of agricultural land was bringing some changes. We were mindful of Sr Duarte's warning when we first arrived that much of the area was within weeks of being sold to a large developer who planned to drain the marshes for two golf courses and to build a large hotel on the botanically important area to the south of the peninsula. It had been clear that we might not have much time, and so we decided early on that our role would be to provide accurate information about the ecological value of the area to national campaigners, but not to lead any campaign ourselves. As foreigners we didn't feel it was our business to interfere in what were national decisions, but we hoped we could help those decisions to be well informed. The issue wasn't completely straightforward; the majority of those involved in altering the face of the Algarve were not Portuguese either, but until A Rocha took on a more national character we felt that it was the only wise approach.

In the event that first threat of development had receded even before we bought Cruzinha, but not before we had been approached to give it a kind of legitimacy by agreeing to work from a study centre which would be provided for us within the development. At a stage when A Rocha was so insubstantial we were surprised to be consulted at all, and it was the first indication that even studying the area could change the way that people thought about it. Needless to say the plan would

138

have been an environmental disaster and all we could do was say so, and politely refuse to endorse it in any way.

In the months that followed we met several other people who had an interest in the proposals, some within the government itself. In the face of the vast sums of money that were being quoted, we felt very insignificant, and there seemed little we could do to influence the inevitable decision for urbanisation, except to pray for the protection of all that was of value to God in the local community and the physical environment.

The turning point came as Cruzinha's second year began to draw to a close, with a phone call from a landscape architect recently graduated from Evora University. His name was Zé Vieira, and on a recent television programme he explained how it happened. "I was very active in nature conservation at college, but when I came to live in the Algarve I felt very isolated. I knew no one here who cared about such things, then someone told me about A Rocha and I just showed up. I was amazed at all the different people who I met here, all with different interests, botanists, ornithologists, entomologists, ecologists . . . I have been coming here all the time ever since!" Zé is a fanatic for 2CV cars, kayaks, computers and wildlife, and he took up the cause of the estuary with complete enthusiasm. A few months after he first visited us, we went together to Lisbon to talk at the first national conference on protected areas, and to plead the cause of the estuary and its marshes. Suddenly there was an outlet for the information we had been gathering on wader migration, plant communities, and the value of the area to the local schools and their teachers. All the studies pointed to an urgent need for the estuary to be preserved.

Together with some of his friends Zé formed a local branch of the Liga para a Protecção da Natureza, Portugal's senior conservation organisation, and one of their first initiatives was to organise a campaign to classify the area as a reserve. Almost immediately it began to have an effect, and we did what we could to support the effort they were making. Zé was able to organise paid leave from his job for a couple of months and took over a room at Cruzinha while he and a colleague prepared an appeal to the European Community for help. Funding for that came from the owners of a local magazine and newspaper who had recently become Christians. Their papers were not the only ones to feature the Liga's campaign and the ripples began to spread quite widely. When Prince Philip had dinner in Lisbon with President Soares and Prime Minister Cavaco Silva, one of his first questions was about the fate of the estuary: he was assured that it would be protected. By the end of the first two months of the campaign it had become impossible for the local authorities to ignore the value of the area, and they classified it as out of bounds to developers. At the time of writing the area remains unprotected, but undeveloped, and a national campaign has just been launched to include the estuary in the national reserves network. A journalist from the national daily *Público* stood here recently looking over the fields towards the sea and said, "This area is a miracle," perhaps unaware of the literal truth of her words.

When Zé first contacted us he was clearly an answer to many prayers, although, as he told us, he had no particular commitment as a Christian at the time. Time and again we have seen that God is the Lord of all people and all things, and not just at work in the church or where he is recognised and acknowledged. It has given us confidence to pray, because there is no limit to his sphere of activity. On many occasions we have seen that only prayer will make a difference, because inventiveness and energy have come to the end of what they can achieve.

The campaign for the estuary, and the increasing number of A Rocha reports about different aspects of the Algarve's environment, led in time to a far greater contact with other conservation groups. We shared similar aims, and so we were frequently asked why we felt it necessary to adopt a distinctively Christian approach to nature conservation. As A Rocha's concern has always been for the applied end of the problem, at first sight there could appear to be little that was distinctive about the environmental work we were doing. Obviously Christians have no monopoly on truth, or on ethical behaviour. Neither is the Christian commitment of a biologist or an ecologist working in conservation necessarily a guarantee that the quality of his work will be higher than that of his uncommitted colleagues. Why then does it matter what he believes, or what an organisation believes, as long as the work is done well?

In answering the question a distinction must be made between the contribution of the Christian community, and the work of individual Christians, but we have come to see that a Christian organisation can contribute in three different ways.

First, we can work to make it acceptable to talk about belief in the context of conservation. When conservationists make a case for the protection of a marsh that is faced with drainage, or a woodland that is to be felled for new housing, they must eventually move beyond a simple description of the habitat. As we have found with the Alvor estuary, it is one thing to identify the species present in the area, to catalogue and classify them according to various criteria, but sooner or later the discussion must go on to the reasons behind the different proposals. Often it is at this point that the lack of an agreed set of values or beliefs becomes most apparent. For a conservationist, it is sufficient to describe the presence of a particular population of orchids on a heath, or the importance of a wood

141

for Nightingales, and he feels his case is made. However, for a local councillor, or the planning authority, it is enough to recognise that the area can be used for creating employment, or contributing to the local economy, for an equal and opposite case to be made. The conflict arises because neither conservationist nor councillor recognises that their descriptions carry no imperative for those on the other side. The argument begins with description, but ends in mutual frustration, because the values and beliefs guiding each side are never explained. Furthermore, they may not even be clear to those involved.

In the relativistic climate of Europe, it is increasingly unacceptable to appeal to belief as a basis for action, and pseudo objectivity is presented as a basis for resolving conflict. It is thought to be enough to establish criteria in legislation, and then the problems can be solved. The difficulty of course is that such criteria are frequently arbitrary, and themselves reflect a series of values that have never been fully articulated or agreed. So the first contribution that Christians can make is to challenge the taboo, and give a clear witness to the need for everyone, Christian or not, to recognise and evaluate the beliefs which motivate us all, rather than to allow them to remain inarticulate, or to be thought irrelevant.

From time to time we are asked to speak about the birds of the Algarve, or conservation in the area. Invariably we explain why A Rocha is working here, and not just what it has been studying. It is important to examine the unspoken assumptions that motivate our work, but this is true for any organisation, and not just those with an explicit Christian commitment. Secular organisations campaigning for wildlife appeal to values all the time, and yet compared with the professionalism of their presentation, and the quality of their scientific research, these vague explanations are often painfully inadequate. In the end the case for conservation is impoverished by the lack of a coherent set of values. Concepts such as beauty or rarity are mobilised, but they are hopelessly relative in the absence of a firm belief in a personal God. Moral judgments are not free-standing, but proceed from beliefs.

142

A recent passage from a conservation magazine was arguing for the protection of Hen Harriers on grouse moors:

> Conservationists argue that the Harrier is a scarce bird in Britain. People want to see them alive and the uplands would be the richer if the marvellous sight of their spring sky-dances were there for more people to see ... As long as the pressure of illegal persecution of Hen Harriers and other protected birds continues, it is very difficult for sporting and conservation camps to make common cause. Without common cause, loss of moorland to farming or forestry will continue, with both sport and wildlife the losers. With it there is the prospect that the combined strengths of the sporting and conservation lobbies could defend their common interests.

In the absence of any agreed values, the argument is reduced to the level of what people want and can benefit from. Not only is this purely anthropocentric, and so inadequate for the many situations where humans cannot be seen to derive any benefit from their protection of the natural world, but also it sees conservation as a simple power struggle between interest groups (in this case either sporting and conservation, or farming and forestry). Inevitably such a struggle means that the most powerful group wins, regardless of whether there is any virtue in what they believe.

If we persist in living as though our beliefs were a matter of private conviction and have no public relevance, we inevitably fall into this kind of incoherence, and yet we encounter that idea more commonly than any other when the Christian basis of A Rocha's work is explained. More than that, since we first began the project, people seem to have become more tolerant of what others believe, but less able to accept that those beliefs might be relevant to anyone else. The Christian beliefs of the team at A Rocha may be thought to be quite sincere but, it seems, definitely their own business.

Secondly, Christians can demonstrate that in biblical truth there is a coherent and firm basis for understanding and

143

evaluating the different claims that are made upon the earth by all its inhabitants, human and otherwise. It is the responsibility of the Christian community to present and embody those beliefs in an accessible form. In any environmental decision, there will inevitably be conflicts of interest, and hard decisions for which it will be impossible to make perfect judgments. Nevertheless the resources for finding a way through the dilemmas are in the fear of the Lord, the beginning of wisdom. Correspondingly it is clear that the earth is damaged by the folly which is godlessness. The prophet Hosea spells it out: "There is no acknowledgement of God in the land . . . because of this the land mourns and all who live in it waste away, the beasts of the field and the birds of the air, and the fish of the sea are dying."

To insist on the practical aspect of this again, it is not possible, or at all desirable, to impose Christian belief on the wider community. In contemporary Britain we will wait a long time for a clear statement of the honour due to the Creator in an editorial of a conservation magazine. Individual Christians who work within secular organisations cannot expect their own beliefs to be thought relevant by their relativist and pragmatic employers. But first we must put our own house in order, and we are a long way from that. Practical Christian initiatives in caring for the earth can be counted on the fingers of one hand.

As we waited to take possession of Cruzinha seven years ago I was researching an article and was unable to find any practical work being undertaken by any Christian church or organisation beyond some tree-planting projects being carried out by Mennonites in Haiti, a Tear Fund project in Honduras, and A Rocha. There had been conferences and books, but no action. More recently events have taken a turn for the better reflecting a sharp rise in environmental awareness in society as a whole. Nevertheless it is still the case that Christian institutions often unthinkingly adopt the damaging lifestyles of their secular counterparts, and churches do not encourage their members to reconsider the way they live in the light of the biblical directive to care for the earth. So until we are demonstrating in practical ways how Christian living is environmental good sense, we will have little to say. It is tragic to reflect on what shape the Industrial Revolution might have taken had the church of the time been faithful to a biblical lifestyle and witness, and better able to guide the development of industry, and the transformation of the landscape, in ways that honoured the Creator and protected his creation.

Thirdly, the church can itself develop distinctive projects that reflect God's concern for the earth which, although belonging to him, is entrusted to our care. However, we must be clear about why we are undertaking such projects. Francis Schaeffer, with his concern for relevant evangelism, rightly perceived that the current absence of Christian organisations from any active environmental work was a lost evangelistic opportunity: "When modern young people have a real sensitivity to nature, they turn to the hippy communities or mentality ... they have seen that most Christians simply do not care about the beauty of nature, or nature as such." However, Schaeffer went on to point out that our motivation is far more than that: "If I am going to be in the right relationship with God, I should treat the things he has made in the same way he treats them."

We are not working at A Rocha because by doing so we can impress visiting conservationists so that they will reconsider the claims of the gospel. We can find our model in Jesus's ministry of healing. He did not heal for evangelistic effect, but out of compassion and because people were sick. Nevertheless the healing work which he did was an embodiment and context for his proclamation of the gospel because it spoke eloquently of the character of God. We must be careful not to create a false polarity, because obedience to the Creator cannot imply neglect of any part of his creation, but we undertake our work in conservation first for the Creator, and with the prime objective of caring for what he has made, and only secondarily for the benefits it may bring to the church's witness. Furthermore, while there is an increasing understanding of the importance of environmental work in Christian circles, I sense that a true conviction of the importance of the Creation to God, aside from its importance for human well-being and survival, is a further step towards a fully biblical view that remains to be taken.

We have endeavoured to embody some of these ideas in our work around the Alvor estuary. The usual conflicts of interest can be clearly seen. Sr Duarte's farm on the shores of the estuary includes some beautiful areas of marsh and scrub. Many other landowners also live in Lisbon, and are anxious to benefit from the high prices being offered for land by property developers. This has always been unprofitable land, and now the workers have found jobs in the local hotels which pay far better. Although they are sad to see the land abandoned, and the vineyards on which they have spent many years overgrown, they do not regret the change. Meanwhile the Ports Department puts forward a plan for development which means that public money would do much of the work of transforming the estuary into a marina.

The local community of fishermen wish to continue with their livelihood, but nearly all are at retirement age, and fish stocks have declined rapidly all along the coast because of overfishing by the Spanish and others offshore. Because the estuary has been silting up, they welcome the initial dredging which is presented as a plan to enable them to get their boats out to sea more easily. No one explains whether they will still have access to the sea if a marina is completed. The Ports Department are able to establish a major work of civil engineering, and to sell the sand from the dredging which they dump on top of the dune system despite their declared intention to pump it on to the beach. In order to get the sand out they build a big road through the dunes, and another across the open estuary. Inland a quarry sells huge blocks of stone for breakwaters at the outlet to the sea. Many people from the nearby villages use the area both for leisure – fishing, collecting shellfish and swimming in the summer – and for their livelihood, as the estuary still provides shellfish in commercial quantities, and is an important source of bait for the fishermen. Some see a tourist development there as progress and would like to see a two-lane asphalt road with streetlights and cafés replacing the earth lane that runs from the village to the shore.

Some feel that the Algarve has lost more than it has gained through tourism. A growing number of people in the nearby towns are beginning to recognise another vocation for the area as a resource for schools, and as a beautiful stretch of

countryside to visit in newly acquired cars at the weekend. One or two even perceive it as a rare habitat in need of protection.

In all this debate it can be seen that the truth of the matter is very hard to obtain. The official bodies rarely act on their declared intentions, or make plain their real reasons for acting. As we have considered how Christians might contribute, we have seen that our actions can be biblical only if decisions are made on the basis of the truth. We have therefore tried to clarify through the meetings to which we have been invited, and through local friends who are members of the committees that make decisions, what in fact is true or false about the different claims that are made. Of course it is not always possible to discover, or to be certain, but it is a good place to start.

For our own part we have studied the area's birds and ecology to discover what is the real contribution that it makes to the environment. Are there good reasons for it remaining in its present state? Could it be improved as a natural habitat? What changes are taking place and why? We have worked to make the results of these studies widely available to national and local planners. Yet again we have found that the hard reality of nature conservation is many hours in the office pushing paper, a far cry from the romantic picture of the lone figure in a faded denim shirt and binoculars out in the wide open spaces. It is worth it to establish the truth.

In discussion with different people who have come to see what we are doing, we have tried to open the issue beyond what is intended, to why it is intended. In the village we have asked people why they feel that tourist development is a good idea. Is the belief that being richer will make you happier well founded? Does it matter that the traditional patterns of family life have been completely disrupted? Does all that has arrived with the tourists represent progress? It is only a case of asking the questions, because the answers have to come from within the community itself, and we genuinely do not have them in any form that can be applied here. Many people have escaped from serious hardship and poverty by means of the wealth that the tourist boom has brought to their families. Our own experience of the place is as very recent arrivals. Nevertheless we hope to be a means whereby the truth of what is happening here can be made plain.

We had seen the second part of a Christian approach as that of developing a clear Christian statement and demonstrating that a biblical approach can work. In a recent meeting where the plans to establish a natural reserve were discussed it became clear that local people assumed there would be a conflict if they continued to work in the area. Biblically, however, there are no necessary grounds for such conflict between

148

human activity and the environment, and there is a framework for reconciling all the different needs. Furthermore, there is a conviction that peace can be made and solutions can be found, and this can go a long way towards overcoming the pessimism which often overwhelms those who are closely observing what is happening to the world around them. There are many reasons for despair in view of the drastic damage that is being inflicted on every side. Even so we were interested when Zé remarked recently that although he arrived in the Algarve with a strong commitment to protecting what remains of its natural habitats, he would have given up long ago if it had not been for A Rocha. This had nothing to do with our setting a particularly inspiring example; it was because we could see that if God had made the world not just for people, or just for wildlife, then there had to be ways through the apparent conflicts of interest, and so there were grounds for not losing hope. Furthermore, we carry on working, not because of a guarantee of success, or a belief that we will change the world, but because it is right to do what we do. E. F. Schumacher put it neatly when he wrote: "We must do what we conceive to be the right thing and not bother our heads or burden our souls with whether we're going to be successful."

The third part of the process has been between us and God, and it goes back to what we have already identified as the spiritual element in environmental destruction. The only way to tackle problems of that nature is with the spiritual resources of prayer and obedience which God gives to his people. While others may not feel able to join us in that, there is no harm in their knowing that we feel it to be as important as all the campaigning, and letters, and study. If you like, it relates to what could be called a complete ecology.

In any ecological study the relationships between all the different elements in the natural system are described. Christians believe, however, that there is a fundamental relationship which affects all the others even before we examine the relationships that we find between people and their physical environment. That relationship is the one between us and our Creator, and it is determinative. Our fractured relationship

149

with God leads to the breakdown of our relationship to the world around us, and in turn to disruption throughout the ecosystem. Once restored in Christ it brings the possibility of healing in every area of life, including our environment.

13

"For nature is more various than observation tho' observers be innumerable." – Kit Smart

For many Europeans, economics, architecture, the motor car and the television all conspire against the wonderfully ramshackle and organic creation of larger family units which can include friends and strangers without much inconvenience. So we count ourselves fortunate in being able to exploit the possibilities of a large house and an ancient but capacious minibus, and over the years the family has been made far richer by those who have joined us. "Who's at home?" is usually the first question the children ask as they get off the school bus in the evening.

Rachel first came here because of a passionate interest in conservation. During her stay she told us that she had seen her own parents divorce, and had often been caught up in the conflicts before and since. She enjoyed all the field work she was able to do, and her studies were very rewarding, but she said that what made her time at A Rocha special was being able to belong to an extended family.

Because Rachel has been one among many, few of the ideas that have become embodied in the way we all work at A Rocha are more important to us than the possibilities of what it means to be that kind of family to those who stay here. We have discovered nothing particularly profound except that a married couple, with their children if they have any, but equally without if they haven't, can provide a centre of gravity which can give affection, acceptance and security to all those whom the family welcomes into itself.

While I was training to become a curate we were able to spend some time at St Michael le Belfry in York, the church led by David Watson and others. In part we were interested to find out something of their experience in living in small communities, and so we visited several of the leaders of the households that were then in operation. In those where families were involved, one secret of success was evident from the innovative struggles that were going on, and that was the necessity for a clearly defined central family unit which was then able to keep the boundaries open to outsiders. If the central unit lost its distinctive identity, both adults and children became uncertain. In the case of the children, they needed to know to whom they were answerable. In the case of the adults, tensions and difficulties rapidly overran idealism if some sort of authority structure was not maintained. Where a clear family identity was established with a husband and wife who took responsibility for all that went on in the house, then life was in general harmonious and creative for everyone else.

We took all this very much to heart, and so later, when working in the parish, we aimed to keep our house open to all comers, but on terms we could consciously control, and with an awareness of the effect on us all of those who joined us for greater or lesser periods of time. Recently we have been very moved by reading of Sheila Cassidy's work in a hospice in her excellent book *Sharing the Darkness*. Early in the book she has this to say:

> When I am feeling strong I see patients alone, without my white coat and ask them how they are *feeling* not only physically, but emotionally. I ask them if they are afraid, if they are sad or if they are angry and I ask them how things are at home. This takes time and a lot of emotional energy and I cannot do it for every patient, so I do it for those who seem to need it most. By doing this I am meeting a small fraction of the human needs of the sick for whom I care.

152

On the days when I am not feeling very strong I see people more formally, with a nurse at my side. I ask them about their physical symptoms, and check the progress of the disease. I order investigations, prescribe treatment and then go away and see someone else. That is the way things are. We too are human and, as Eliot says, human kind cannot bear too much reality.

Sheila Cassidy is working in a far more stressful place than we are, and caring for people suffering far more. But there are times and seasons for all those who work in community, and we have found it necessary to be realistic about our limitations, so that we can be sure of sustaining an open lifestyle without burning out. Certainly there is a period of adjustment, but once we are adapted to living closely with others, heroism is of little value, because openness has to be genuine and spontaneous. This means taking into account the different needs and tolerance levels of each member of the family. We rapidly discovered that in our case the children had quite as much to give as we did to those who were with us, and often an astonishing understanding of who was particularly in need of love and affirmation. Because it wasn't conscious or engineered in any way, it meant a great deal to those on the receiving end of three-year-old love. But each had their own way of showing that they had become over-exposed at times, and we learnt to recognise the signals, and to begin a strategic withdrawal on their behalf if necessary. Similarly while we might be frustrated at our own limitations, and wish we had greater energy and capacity to respond to those who share the house, there are times when we feel we have reached saturation point and so we try to withdraw for a while, not to ask too closely about the lives of those who are staying, and to absent ourselves from an evening in the Cruzinha common room because we need space for ourselves. There are also times, of course, when despite those limitations you cannot withdraw, and so accumulate a temporary overdraft on your personal resources, but there are many precedents for that in far more desperate circumstances, from the Apostle Paul to Sheila Cassidy.

We have an architectural witness to these truths in the form of a strange and wonderful door at the top of the Cruzinha spiral staircase. I have never seen such an incongruously placed door, and it took the confidence of a friend who is a civil engineer to give us the courage to put such a narrow and impractical object in. It is amazing that we haven't swept anyone down the stairs as it swings out dangerously over the steep spiral, but so far we've avoided any serious accidents. It marks the entrance to our flat, and often it is left open, but the point is that we can shut it if we want to. There are many leaders and workers who manage without such luxuries, and maybe we could if we had to, but it has been a lifesaver at times. By marking out our own area, it also gives us something of our own to give and to share if we choose which is often an extra joy.

For sheer stress and inconvenience, the people who have joined the family have never been in the same league as all the animals and injured birds that we have accumulated at different times. We have never had anything exotic, although one lady arrived hoping we could sell her a parrot, and the first school group ever to come to Cruzinha, fifty children from the Vila Verde *infantário* who swarmed unannounced up the drive one May morning, made a beeline for the irrigation tank where their teacher had promised them they would definitely see dolphins, if not seals.

Many of the animals arrived because our children combined hopeless optimism about what was required to keep them all fed and happy, with less knowledge of basic biology than you would expect from kids who were growing up in a field centre. When the guinea-pig numbers rose to twenty-three, we insisted that they donated some to friends, and to their hapless parents who were destined to be unwitting observers of the powers of rodent reproductivity. "We'll just take two females," one organised family told us. "Sure," agreed Jeremy, carefully selecting the two that were most heavily pregnant and whistling casually as he placed them comfortably in the immaculate box on the back seat of their car.

The children's ambitions in husbandry acquired the fervour

of a moral crusade when they discovered that our neighbours' fluffy little baby rabbits were all destined for the pot. The crunch came when they managed to name them all through the wire and went each day to visit them, returning to tell us which ones could still be saved by a mercy dash. It gave us a new insight into the significance of the naming of animals in Genesis. Then there was the terrapin found wandering in the street in Portimão, called Quicky Joe by Esther, and Zé Rapido by his Portuguese friends. An attempt was made to breed rare Western Spadefoot Toads by David Rees and his family who were living with us at the time, and they were christened the Wolloes by Bethan who was confused by the young swallows fledging in the outhouse. We did, however, draw the line at the skeleton of a mule that Jeremy wished to bring home from a Spanish hillside for re-assembly in his bedroom. The final deal was that he could have the femur as a doorknocker, but that he must leave the rest for the vultures.

We've never had a vulture, but some of the other birds have been spectacular. Foia the buzzard was found staggering along a beach having apparently escaped from some captor, judging by the string trailing from her leg. News of her attacks on the smaller members of the family and on the younger visitors was greeted with unsympathetic excitement as she recovered her fighting spirit. After some weeks with us, when her growing aggression gave encouraging signs that she would manage, she was released into the wild by a local falconer. The huge Eagle Owl, ransomed from people planning to kill her to be stuffed, never looked so likely to manage on her own, but she prowled the common room at night and ate quantities of raw meat until the staff of the recuperation centre in Olhão came to fetch her. They took the White Stork as well, but not our most famous client whose progress to Portugal was followed each night in millions of British homes. This was the Alpine Swift which arrived, accompanied by a BBC film crew, on British Airways flight 518. A few days before it had made an unwise landfall near Spaghetti Junction, a thousand kilometres north of where it should have been, and a compassionate conservation organisation decided to repatriate it in a blaze of

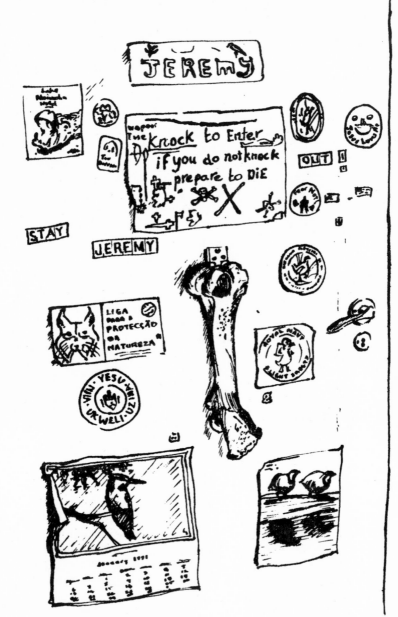

publicity on the nine o'clock news. A stream of phone calls preceded our modest role in the affair. Would we take delivery, and then release the bird? It would come with a few days' supply of meal worms. No, after all it couldn't have any meal worms because that would infringe EEC regulations on the transport of live animals; could we organise some locally? Would we mind recording a brief interview at the airport? When we finally presented ourselves at Faro at the agreed hour, the meaning of the hasty interviews over the closed lid of the box was only too clear. The film crew were well on their way back to the returning plane by the time we loosened all the bird protection stickers and got the box open. We never discovered whether it was stardom or over-rapid reverse migration in a Boeing which had proved fatal, but apparently the final news report was long on local atmosphere, and romantically ambiguous about the bird's future life.

In general the birds have been easier than the dogs. Bonita, who must once have been handsome, was found to be living at the house when we moved in, and is chiefly remembered for surviving Mark's cooking – he cooked half for her and ate the rest himself during the weeks he held the fort on his own. Her successor, Bella, gave us some awkward moments with our neighbours because of her passion for takeaway chicken, and the speed with which she dashed into their yards before the final burst of feathers gave a whole new meaning to the term fast food. Very sadly she succumbed to sandfly fever which is a great problem for dogs in the south of Iberia. She is buried along with Sunday Mallard, and three of the rabbits, Candy, Bobbin and Venture, who survived myxomatosis only to be eaten by stray dogs who tore up their hutch one stormy night. Their graveyard was constructed along Pre-Raphaelite lines by the children, and was adorned by Jo with tremulous messages on odd pieces of local marble: "Candy, Bobbin and Venture – Killed by Dogs after Bravely Recovering from a Dreaded Disease – Fondly Remembered. 1988".

Currently we have a loopy mongrel who was born on a local beach and is mostly a great disgrace. We have become progressively more sceptical of the myths about canine

157

intelligence and instinct as she stumbles over her own paws and develops new antisocial habits daily. Life is never dull for Esther who is her nominal owner, and who therefore has the task of explaining her more bizarre behaviour. At present we are battling with her love for joining in our Sunday worship with a chilling soprano howl. If we forget to warn visitors they can be seen to undergo conflicting emotions until they realise that it is only the dog. She has recently been joined by an Algarve water dog, a rare local breed only recently rescued from the brink of extinction which Ze has persuaded us to accept on the basis that they have webbed feet, and are therefore sufficiently like ducks to be acceptable in a bird observatory. This preoccupation with saving disappearing species can sometimes colour the children's view of life in too zoological a fashion. We overheard a visitor asking Jeremy if he had great-grandparents. "No," he told them, "they're extinct."

As the months passed, the number of people who came to work on the team at Cruzinha gradually grew. By the end of 1990 there were seven of us, and although our family were the only ones to be living permanently in the house, while the others had rooms or flats in the village, the A Rocha team was functioning more and more as a small community, rather than as an extended family. As a rather specific community, gathered around a shared, if very varied, commitment to biblical Christianity and a range of environmental interests, we could not appeal to any similar institution for many of the patterns we adopted as we endeavoured to live out the gospel together. This brought us both real advantages, and a greater cost.

Among the advantages was that we were able to adapt very easily to the different needs of all the visitors who came to join us at Cruzinha. The numbers had gradually risen until each year nearly a thousand came to see what we were doing, and around two hundred and fifty stayed for different periods of time. Often they were with us during a Sunday, and on that day we were able to work from first principles about the need and privilege of worship, the need to rest and to take time out

158

from work, the need to be with each other without chasing the clock. No two Sundays were the same, and the fact that we had no standard agreed form was a great benefit. Those who were with us might never have been in any worship before, or might have been out on the marsh from dawn, or might need to catch a train mid-morning. There was always the risk of someone arriving during the service to announce that they had found some rare wader nearby, and always the possibility of an eagle flying over if we were meeting outside in the autumn or spring. When we met for worship, the team could not adopt an inaccessible public persona; it was simply us, and we contributed what we could. As we prepared, we learned who tended to be good at what, who could play an instrument for the singing, who taught the Bible well, who could be relied on to direct the course of our worship sensitively. Halfway through we stopped to put the lunch on.

The reason that we have found it at times more costly, compared to our experience of leading a church, is that at each point there are far more decisions to be made. How were we to spend those Sundays so that we found what we needed in them, and were true to what God expected of them? There were no expectations from any congregation to meet, but we had to be endlessly flexible. A little routine might have been a relief on the days when we felt exhausted or unable to give of our best, and there were no robes or white coat for protection on the days when we felt vulnerable.

Despite that greater vulnerability, and despite the fact that our worship was less even and predictable as a result, the continuity of worship with everyday things could be very evident to us all. As those who stayed in the house came to know us first in the context of ringing, or plant studies, or practical environmental work of different kinds, and only later in the context of the beliefs that informed it all, they encountered those beliefs with some personal identity already established, and with some way of evaluating what they meant in practice.

There is a more institutional context for the monthly service in the village, by virtue of the fact that we must fix a common time and rent a room. The decision to meet on a Sunday as the beginnings of a Lusitanian Church developed quite naturally from the Bible studies, and so far it has been very rewarding. Even there, however, we are working at making it as personal and informal as possible, and so the preaching is actually a kind of dialogue at times, the liturgy is very simple, and we avoid any jargon or religiosity at all. In Vila Verde I'm known as Sr Peter who runs the bird study centre, not as a minister or anyone professionally religious. My interest in getting people to worship God together is seen as part of me (perhaps a very strange part) and not the way I earn my living. If I were to wear special clerical clothing it would give people a terrible shock – which is a good job because my robes disappeared into the children's dressing-up box some time ago. In practice it is Miranda who invites more people to come, because she is in the village most days, and spends a lot of time talking and often praying with friends or visiting different people she knows; so the service is recognised as something that comes from our family and friends, and not as an institutional event. We try to keep it all in the context of the friendships we have during the rest of the week. In a culture where religion is recognised as an entirely separate activity proper to women and children, this is so important. I am pessimistic about the chances of being able to sustain such a style as numbers grow, but it will be worth fighting for.

It was Luis who said it, but it could have been any one of a hundred visitors to A Rocha. "To be honest, believing in God isn't anything I've ever really thought about before. I'm not religious, you see." Slight pause: "My mother was . . ."

If we are to face the fact that the vast majority of Europeans find the church completely irrelevant, then we must listen to what they say to find out why. The problem is that very often we no longer know what questions to ask, because we have learned to tolerate the way that many churches are so far removed from normal life. In learning how to worship at A Rocha we have wanted to emulate those churches which are striving to remove religious jargon and arcane practice from their expression of worship. In response to what we have heard from many people about the church, we have struggled to make our worship at A Rocha wholehearted, straightforward and uncluttered and have found that for some of those who have joined us it is a revelation. Jorge was one of them. "I have never in all my life been to anything like that before. Do you do that every Sunday? Do all of you who live here believe?" And so the discussion continued.

Perhaps we are tempted to wrap worship in special language and special behaviour because we are uncomfortable with the plain presence of God in every part of our lives, and the force of the gospel to speak to everything we are, and all that we do. Whatever the reason, we now face a creative challenge if we want to express our life in Christ in a way that does justice both to our longing to be in the presence of God, and our friends' surprise that it is possible. Our wrappings have led people to expect the Christian life to be complicated but easy, while in reality it is simple, but can be terribly difficult.

Through living in a place where people come to you rather than you going to them, we have come to realise that we are very dependent on God to bring the right people at the right time. We have a house rule that we give a welcome to everyone on the basis that in practice you can't do much else by the time they have actually arrived. Again there is a deep biblical truth in the idea of unconditional acceptance, and it has at times sustained us through some of the more unexpected vagaries that we encounter in our guests. Even so Sarah had a struggle to accept one keen birder who was so enthusiastic to communicate his observations at great length that he followed her into the bathroom to which she had fled in a desperate attempt to escape the unstoppable torrent of data.

While it is testing to work in a project for which there is no clear precedent, it has the great advantage that you can derive what you do very directly from the aims that you have. You inherit no traditions, and there are no expectations to meet. Both in establishing the church, and in the daily work of the centre, we have been able to build around the intentions that we have. We are fortunate in this, but as some of our more successful ideas become customary, and then no doubt almost

161

traditional, we will need to hang on to the need to be radical. It must always be a useful exercise to stand back and decide what it is you intend to do, and then to look hard at how you actually spend your time. Do our way of life and worship serve our intentions, or are they simply inherited, or expected of us? We may have to compromise, but at least we should do so consciously and not drift into it by historical accident. Even so, we have often had insufficient creativity or energy to shape our own work as well as we could, and we have certainly made some mistakes along the way. Usually it has been by depriving people of an opportunity for reaching out to God that they would have appreciated. Miranda's instinct for who will be glad if we offer to pray for them, or who will want to join us if we are ending a meal with some readings and singing, has usually been vindicated in the face of my reticence and over-caution. Precisely because her role at A Rocha is less clearly defined she is usually able to drop everything to spend time with people who call unexpectedly.

One final observation about family and community. In a family, even if someone behaves in an unacceptable way, he or she remains your relation. The ties cannot be severed. Sometimes in order to limit the damage, people must distance themselves from their relations, but they remain family. So it is with other Christians. We may not like each other or agree with each other but we are drawn together. There can be that element of discipline in community and team work. It is wonderful if deep friendship develops, but it isn't necessarily to be expected, and we have all found a spectrum of sympathy among those who join us for different periods of time. The basis for being together is calling, and not preference. What is certain, and again it reflects something of the relationship that God has with us, is that you become very known by those you work with in community, and get to know them uncomfortably well too.

We have found this to be in marked contrast to some urban professional churches, where the relationship between people can often be more like the collision of billiard balls than Juan Carlos Ortiz's famous image of mashed potato. In an impersonal city everybody is working under great pressures of time, and needs to protect him- or herself against aggression and exploitation. It is not surprising that the instinct for self-defence soon becomes part of church relationships too. Perhaps churches that are rooted in big cities, or competitive sub-cultures, have a particular need to establish community relationships within the church, because in a working community it is impossible to remain incognito or inscrutable. Inevitably at Cruzinha we let each other and ourselves down, but that fact has to be faced, and there is no hope of avoiding people until it can be forgotten. We have found that the disappointment if someone wounds you is akin to the disappointment you feel about yourself when you fail. If we fail, we do not easily dismiss ourselves; instead our first instinct is to excuse our failure and to remain loyal. We have to carry on inside our own skin and so we can overcome our failure. Similarly in the enforced commitment of community, there is a profound challenge to our instinct to categorise and dismiss that which we find difficult in someone else.

In Charlie Cleverly's book *Church Planting, Our Future Hope* he has recommended that we choose to work with those who are like-minded. This has caused some discussion here, but it seems to be wise advice, and having battled at times with our differences, we would now do all we could to avoid unnecessary pain by following it. Nevertheless there will also be times when God so clearly chooses the people with whom you will live and work that the rule goes by the board, and then it is best to realise what it is you are being called to and not to have unrealistic expectations of deep friendship. So many important insights about the gospel seem to be taught by living in community, that a degree of community commitment ought surely to be part of any church's life? It is probably not an accident that as Europe takes leave of God it travels further down the road to social fragmentation and isolation. As our churches take root in this culture, they will have to fight all the harder for the importance of community. Sometimes they will fail. Many churches in Portugal have bowed to the inevitable, and schedule their meetings for late at night after the

Brazilian soap operas are finished. But if we do not insist on the fundamental nature of community for the expression of the Christian life we will not only fail to understand each other, we will fail to understand God.

14

"He has also set eternity in the hearts of men; yet they cannot fathom what God has done from beginning to end." – Ecclesiastes

Vila Verde station has been the venue for some historic moments in A Rocha's past. It is flanked by palm trees, and has a wonderfully nineteenth-century air with its dignified, square building, and the heavy pots of plants on the platform. Special features include the sign that declares it to be Vila Verde which is tucked so high up into the roof that it is invisible to anyone on the train. As a result many of our visitors continue on to Lagos where the line ends, and then return in the opposite direction half an hour later. Rosário Pereira had been warned, however, and so got off first time through.

Rosário is a marine biologist from Porto, and her arrival at the beginning of 1991 as our first full-time Portuguese team member marked the beginning of present times for A Rocha. Since then she has been joined by Paula Banza and by Marcial Felgueiras, but Rosário was the first answer to many prayers. We had continued to pray for Portuguese colleagues to join the team at Cruzinha, but rarely met any Christian students with an interest in environmental work. So when Rosário wanted to join us we saw it as something remarkable.

There is a fine balance in these matters, because we know that in Christ nationality is not a significant issue. Paul says there is no Jew and no Greek. Nevertheless a national Christian has great advantages in understanding the significance of the

gospel for his or her own culture. No foreigner can easily match the ability to communicate enjoyed by someone who works in his or her own language, or can perceive by instinct the reservations people have when they meet new ideas. Portuguese people are famous for their warm appreciation of foreigners, and so the fact that we are British never seemed too great a handicap in the early years of A Rocha. Nevertheless it was always a provisional state of affairs until we could be joined by national colleagues.

Once Colin has left the team will be made up of three of us who are British, and three who are Portuguese. Earlier this year (1992) a national committee began to take over some of the decision-making. Our family expects to leave within the next few years so that the leadership of Cruzinha can be transferred. Undoubtedly there will be times when we will not find it easy to hear about the direction that the project may have taken, because by definition we would have done things differently, but the genius of national decision-making is precisely that. One of the differences is that the project will certainly be better adapted to local needs, even though we gather that the national leadership is keen to retain the international character of Cruzinha. In this too some important biblical thinking is expressed. We see the confidence with which Jesus entrusted the message of the Kingdom of God to his disciples, and the apparently cavalier fashion in which Paul preached and established a small church, and then appointed leaders and moved on leaving them to work out the local implications and forms (albeit with much heartache at times). By contrast we can be tempted to hang on to influence for fear of what might happen if we were to entrust the future to the Holy Spirit working through local leaders.

Present days at Cruzinha are in some ways not so different from the beginning when the first visitors arrived and threw down their rucksacks in the bedrooms by the common room. We are still battling to find room for Portuguese students who turn up without warning in a week booked months before by birders from the north of Europe. An Avocet and a Hen Harrier are currently stored in the freezer, although the ban on snakes in the fridge has held. The latest generation of improbable traps, this time designed to catch Moorhens and Water Rails for ringing, has been pressed into service to capture a rat seen by the washroom so that it can be deported. So far the most popular suggestion for its eventual destination is around the night club that keeps everyone awake until 4 a.m. in August. The estuary is still undeveloped although still officially without protection. There is talk of it being classified a national nature reserve later this year, and the Liga have mounted an impressive campaign with beautiful posters.

Outwardly the house is unchanged, although we dismantled the artificial storks' nest on the roof after it was colonised by sparrows instead – a disadvantage if you make your tea with rainwater. Instead there is a beautiful Hoopoe weather-vane made by two recent volunteers, Camilla and Esther, and a far less beautiful but very useful radio mast that we set up late one evening while Miranda was in the UK. "And I sat up on the roof all night with Dad," reported Bethan rather disastrously on her return. And yet although the house looks much the same, we have seen some progress in the work that Cruzinha was established to do. Following a couple of television programmes, and quite a few articles in magazines and newspapers, more people throughout the country know about A Rocha, and our visitors these days are as likely to be Portuguese as British, German, Dutch or Finnish.

The sudden rise in the number of Finns was quite a surprise until we discovered that someone had published a book in Helsinki that identified Cruzinha's garden as the only place in Portugal to see Waxbills. We're always glad to meet more Finns, but never know whether to explain to those who have made Cruzinha a place of pilgrimage on their way to a complete European list of species that they can see Waxbills in a thousand other places in Portugal. Rosário has taken some time to get used to the preference of the Finnish birder for battle gear, and told us that she thought the third world war had begun when she saw the first group swarming up from the car park in khaki fatigues festooned with optical equipment of bazooka proportions. In order not to be diverted from our principal work in the Portuguese community we keep Thursday lunchtimes for casual callers from elsewhere who want to know where to go birding or to visit Cruzinha, and most of the time it seems to work.

The initial uncertainty that we encountered from officialdom has been replaced by solid support. Local councils have supported one or two projects such as the production of reports, and we were even visited by a presidential candidate in the run-up to the last elections.

The schools work is now continuous and Paula and Rosário have developed a good programme of activities to guide the teachers. In the education room, Zé Manuel's pride and joy even without the stairs across the windows, there are beautiful display panels painted by Mark, Colin and Will showing the local habitats and their plants and birds. Another shows some of the results of the ringing programme with birds that have come bearing rings from all over Europe, more than a hundred in all. We now ring over seven thousand birds a year of more than a hundred species; some of them have been found in Senegal, Morocco, Germany and Ireland among other places. Best of all so far are the two Storm Petrels, never before ringed in Portugal, which were subsequently caught in Shetland. Mark is now doing post-doctoral research on Storm Petrels up there, although we told him not to go to such trouble just for us. He is married to Jane who passed Maria's critical inspection. Colin is off to Bible college, and is wondering if he might return to East Africa maybe to help establish an A Rocha centre there. Rosário is dreaming dreams of similar work in the north of Portugal and we are wondering about Turkey or Italy . . .

I was asked to go to Guinea Bissau with Marcial to speak to church leaders about nature conservation among other things, and we can see that there is a rapid awakening in the church worldwide to the urgent need to be active in protecting God's earth. Things have changed enormously since the first days when the more normal reaction to the idea of Christian involvement was incomprehension. Each year we publish the results of the field work, which now encompasses botany, geography and marine biology as well as ornithology, and the reports go to government departments and universities. Even with Gonçalo at the helm, translation is still a headache, but now it is in both directions.

Among the other publications is a careful account of all the moths and butterflies of the study area, produced after a six-month study by another volunteer warden, Adrian Gardiner. The field work nearly came to an abrupt end at 3 a.m. one night when Adrian brought the trap out to catch moths at Ponta da Piedade while we were catching Storm Petrels. The birds only come to land at night, and in order to bring them close to the nets we were playing a tape of their calls from an enormous loudspeaker wired in to the lighthouse. Apart from bringing in seabirds, the appalling din attracted the local *Guarda* who stumbled on the bright light from the trap as they came to investigate. When Adrian

appeared out of the darkness he found them with their rifles trained on his precious lamp. They were understandably jumpy, and it took some time to persuade them that the *son et lumière* was all in the interests of science.

That was not the last occasion when the cacophony of Storm Petrel tapes has lifted a night at the coast above the ordinary. Just a few weeks ago Colin went out towards midnight with five members of the Wash Wader Group who had come to help us with the ringing of the many Knot and Dunlin that pass through on their way north each spring. While they were setting up the nets on the open estuary a *Guarda* patrol came across the ringing equipment and packets of rings that they had left on the beach. It probably didn't help that some of the bags we use to keep the birds in originally belonged to a bank and have "£100 SILVER" written on them. Assuming the strange collection of flasks of coffee, old bird bags, gas lamps, shoes and odd bits of clothing to be related to some form of drug smuggling they were gingerly lifting it all into their Land-Rover when Alison, one of the group who had been setting a net for Storm Petrels further along the beach, switched on the tape. As the notorious calls filled the night air, the *Guarda* took it for a motorboat making a getaway, and their *Capitão* fired into the air to summon reinforcements. Colin and the others rushed over to the flashing lights and shouts to find Alison surrounded by eight policemen armed with semi-automatic weapons and fairly terrified – ornithology in Lincolnshire isn't usually half as exciting. Once Colin had produced a marginally relevant piece of paper which a Lisbon office had given to a visiting ringer some years before and which we had kept ever since for a moment like this, it all calmed down, but they insisted he went into Portimão with them to make a statement. Comic relief was provided by the ensuing search for the keys of their Land-Rover which had been dropped somewhere in the dunes in all the excitement, and their demonstrations of how they had moved the ringing gear like high explosive into the vehicle. As the Wash Wader Group normally use cannons to fire their nets they were glad they had decided to leave them back in Britain.

By contrast, the conference that gave rise to another of the reports for sale in the education room was a relatively calm affair, probably because it required no field work. It was entitled Caring for God's Earth, and was organised to encourage Christian thinking about the urgent issues which helped to bring A Rocha into being. The report includes contributions from all our Council and several others, and is a useful complement to the other more scientific publications.

Mark's winter atlas is now in its second edition and still going strong. Bob's work on the wetlands of the Western Algarve has been supplemented by another on the *barrocal*, limestone areas which have suffered dramatic changes as new roads and quarries push inland from the coast. The reports mean that there is no lack of information when decisions must be made about altering the landscape in different ways. Recently we have been asked by two developers to advise them on how to protect the areas they are working in so that they can minimise the environmental impact of what they want to do. Even three years ago, they would never have bothered.

The church in the village looks more like a going concern and will soon be under the care of Paul and Nikki McVeagh who have moved from England to take it on and begin another in Portimão. Like us they were working on Merseyside and have three small children, and so history repeats itself. We had to sigh when we heard that shortly before they were due to leave for Portugal one of their children was rushed to hospital when a mysterious but sizeable lump suddenly appeared on the side of her neck. She is now fine, as was Esther who spent a week in the same hospital for a similarly trivial but alarming illness shortly before we came. These are all very familiar disruptions. We still help the GBU but these days instead of the three university groups that existed ten years ago, there are now fifteen. (There are eleven members of the Évora group in the common room as I write, and seven students from Faro have just asked if they can stay for supper which begins in half an hour. *Plus ça change . . .*) Alfredo and Quim whom we first met as second-year students are now part of a national management committee for A Rocha.

172

It hasn't all been easy even in recent times. Two cars have been written off, although miraculously no one was hurt, even on the last occasion when the VW left the road on a corner in heavy rain in the hills and somersaulted then rolled down a thirty-foot drop. We have been saddened by the damage done to the dune system as the dredging of the estuary has progressed, and a new tide of development is threatening even the protected areas of the south-west coast. The magnificent reedbed at Abicada where there were wintering Bluethroats in hundreds, was burned by hunters and then drained so that it no longer exists. Only three reedbeds remain in the western Algarve now, and all of them are under threat.

Another disappointment came when some valued friends joined a church which does not allow them to recognise the members of any other. Many such churches, and other sects that are even more weird and wonderful, are springing up in the religious wasteland of modern Europe. Portugal is not exempt, but there are so few churches giving a clear witness to the gospel that it is hard to bear. Several of those we have talked to over the years are confused by the proliferation of different groups which make it even harder for them to discover what they think about Christian belief.

Someone asked us recently where the greatest stress lay in our lives, and of course it is mostly generated by a lack of faith, and our inability to cope well with some of what we must do. At times we feel completely overwhelmed by visitors, by maintaining the ringing at all hours, preventing the water system from packing up (Portugal is currently enduring its worst drought for a hundred years), responding to requests for data and for collaboration with other people's studies, piles of letters to answer, talks to prepare, the needs of our friends nearby, the necessity to find space to be with God when we are hopelessly short of sleep – in fact by nothing out of the ordinary.

But of course we are here because of all these things, and not in spite of them. We are able to discover something of the grandeur of God because we are so far out of our depth. Our flicker of concern for God's creation stems from the unquenchable flame of love that he bears for it, and so we can be confident that it will be renewed. We live out our darkest days under the bright wings.

In order to write this I have stopped the clock at a certain point in A Rocha's life. I have not done so because we have arrived anywhere in particular. We have a long way to go and will doubtless continue to make many mistakes getting there. But the need for Christian initiatives in environmental work is greater than ever. Worldwide, in nearly every area, the unprotected earth is subject to rapid and ill-judged assault, and yet there is little sign of a prophetic and sacrificial response from the church. Of course in most cases it is the business of governments to regulate what happens in the environment, if they can. However, in that too our God is the Lord. My only intention in recounting our experience is to encourage other Christians to take up the challenge, not least because they can see how partial and limited have been our own efforts. By virtue of God's infinite creativity and compassion, it should not be difficult to discover ways to begin.

Bibliography

The books below are those referred to at different points in *Under the Bright Wings*, together with one or two others which may be of interest for further reading.

Mark Bolton, *An Atlas of Wintering Birds in the Western Algarve* (A Rocha, Portugal, 1989)

Robert Bridges (ed.), *The Poems of Gerard Manley Hopkins* (Oxford University Press, London, 1931)

Sheila Cassidy, *Sharing the Darkness* (Darton, Longman and Todd, London, 1988)

Charlie Cleverly, *Church Planting, Our Future Hope* (Scripture Union, London, 1991)

Tim Cooper, *Green Christianity* (Spire/Hodder and Stoughton, London, 1990)

Vincent Donovan, *Christianity Rediscovered* (SCM, London, 1982)

Ron Elsdon, *Greenhouse Theology* (Monarch, Tunbridge Wells, 1992)

David Jones, *The Anathemata* (Faber and Faber, London, 1952)

David Jones, *Epoch and Artist* (Faber and Faber, London, 1959)

Lars Jonsson, *Birds of the Mediterranean and Alps* (Croom Helm, London, 1982)

Marion Kaplan, *The Portuguese* (Viking, New York, 1991)

C. S. Lewis, *The Screwtape Letters* (Geoffrey Bles, London, 1942)

Rowland Moss, *The Earth in Our Hands* (IVP, Leicester, 1982)

Bob Pullan, *The Wetlands of the Western Algarve* (Liverpool University, Liverpool, 1990)

Francis Schaeffer, *Pollution and the Death of Man* (Hodder and Stoughton, London, 1970)

Brian Stanley, *The Bible and The Flag* (Apollos, Nottingham, 1990)

Ruth Goring Stewart, *Environmental Stewardship* (IVP, Leicester, 1992)

John Stott, *Issues Facing Christians Today* (Marshall, Morgan and Scott, Basingstoke, 1984)

Marcus Walsh (ed.), *Christopher Smart, Selected Poems* (Fyfield Books, Manchester, 1979)

A ROCHA

Christians in Conservation

Postscript

In the years since *Under the Bright Wings* first appeared, A Rocha has grown beyond all expectations! There are now A Rocha projects in seven countries, and several others under discussion. In 1995 the Harris family left Cruzinha, handing over the leadership to Mark and Jane Bolton under the direction of a national committee. Peter and Miranda began an itinerant lifestyle as International Co-ordinators, visiting Christians in different parts of the world who had been inspired by the work at Cruzinha, and wanted to do something similar. It has been an exciting time, as God has opened up new opportunities and provided the necessary leaders and finances. What follows is a brief summary of these newer projects.

Lebanon (established 1997)

The A Rocha team here is working to protect the last major wetland in the country — the Aammiq Marsh, in the Western Bekaa. Each spring and autumn, the marsh is a vital refueling station for thousands of migrant birds: storks, pelicans, waders and passerines, whilst impressive numbers of birds of prey also pass through the valley. Until recently, the marsh was threatened with destruction by tenant farmers who annually drained and ploughed new sections, while it became ever more degraded by burning, over-grazing and heavy, indiscriminate hunting. Now, thanks to the vision and full co-operation of the major landowner, the marsh is recovering, and with good management it has the potential to be an increasingly important haven for resident wildlife, as well as for migrant birds and insects. It is also becoming better appreciated as an important resource for the local people, as the team, led by Chris and Susanna Naylor, become involved in environmental education with school children and university students.

France (established 1997)

The Harris family is now based in France, and they continue the work of international co-ordination while working part-time with the team led by Frédéric Baudin. His background as both Mediterranean ecologist and biblical theologian equip him wonderfully for his work as National Director, and he is currently leading a team of five people. During 1999 an exceptionally rich study site was discovered in the Vallée des Baux, near Arles. It includes some of the last remnants of natural wetland in the valley and is a beautiful area, with a wide variety of habitats. Initial studies are underway to survey the plants, birds and insects, in order to gain a greater understanding of the functioning of the marsh.

A programme of outings has begun to introduce local people to the wildlife of the region, and a field study centre is planned for the future.

Kenya (established 1998)

Colin Jackson, one-time Assistant Warden at Cruzinha, returned home to Kenya with the vision for an A Rocha centre in a country where the church is large, and influential, but the Christian understanding of creation care is very limited. Following four years working as an ornithologist training Kenyan staff and students at the national museum he is now based at Watamu, on the coast, where he has begun the process of setting up an environmental education and research centre adjacent to five internationally important sites for biodiversity conservation. There has been a lot of progress in the early months and A Rocha Kenya is now recognised as an NGO by the government. The national committee led by Edwyn Kiptiness is widening the national support base, and Professors George Kinoti, Cal de Witt, and John Stott led a national conference entitled "God's world? God's word?" attended by over 300 people in Nairobi in 1999. Meanwhile, in Watamu, Colin is heavily involved in local wildlife surveys, training programmes and in the leadership of local conservation groups. At present, the accommodation for volunteers and visitors is a small rented house, but Colin hopes to move soon to a fully equipped centre nearby.

UK (established 1999)

From early 2001 there will be a full-time UK Director, the Rev Dave Bookless. Dave is a qualified bird-ringer, having first become interested in wildlife during his childhood in India. After studies in Indian and African history, and theology, he taught for four years in a multi-racial school.

For the last nine years he has been an Anglican minister in Southall, West London, where A Rocha aims to establish the first A Rocha Centre in the UK, as well as a small nature reserve. Southall is a multi-racial and urbanised community, with over 85% of the residents being of South Asian origin and less than 10% having a Christian affiliation. Strong links are developing with Christian environmental projects in India, and Dave and his wife Anne are looking forward to leading a Christian community in a setting which, outwardly, could hardly be more different from Cruzinha. Yet, as new projects have sprung up, common experiences of working as Christians in community, living cross-culturally, prioritising conservation and, when necessary, campaigning for the protection of local habitats has given each project a distinctive A Rocha flavour.

Canada (established 1999)

For several years Peter and Miranda have taught a summer course at Regent College, Vancouver. A group of former students, and others, began to think and pray about the potential for an A Rocha project in Canada, and in 1999 "A Rocha Canada — Christians in Conservation" was accepted by the government as a not-for-profit society. The board members (mostly based on the west coast), have already established their own programme of activities, organise the national membership and are planning towards the establishment of a field study centre.

Czech Republic (established 2000)

The first project in Eastern Europe is just beginning, following a conference in Husinec in June 2000 which brought together university professors and students, pastors, journalists, business people and others from all over the

Republic. Under Pastor Pavel Svetlik's guidance a national committee is coming together to plan for the future.

And in Portugal...

The Trustees' long-cherished hope that Cruzinha would in time be handed over to Portuguese wardens has at last been fulfilled. Marcial Felgueiras has returned, with his wife Paula and their small children, Beatriz and Zé. Marcial also has a new role as National Director, and together with the national committee, he is working to extend A Rocha's influence throughout the country.

Staff and volunteers who have worked hard for many years in surveying and studying the local wildlife and habitats, and campaigning for their protection, are now enjoying the satisfaction of seeing the Alvor estuary designated a Natura 2000 site, in large part due to the scientific information A Rocha has provided.

Other projects are on the horizon, not least in the United States, where as we go to press the process of incorporating A Rocha is just coming to a conclusion. The national board is led by Ginny Vroblesky, who works on a wetland reserve in the Chesapeake Bay, and has a background in environmental policy and as an author. She and national representative Deana Strom are always keen to hear from people in the US interested in what is planned for the coming months, and can be contacted via the address below.

As A Rocha blossoms, there is a need for deep roots to sustain the growth. You can help by becoming a member, and as well as receiving your national news, you will also receive *A Rocha International News* four times a year, keeping you up to date with all the projects.

—Barbara Mearns
A Rocha International Staff Member
September 2000

To receive the latest newsletter,
and a membership form, write to:
A Rocha,
3 Hooper St, Cambridge, CB1 2NZ, England
e-mail: a_rocha@compuserve.com
or phone/fax + 44 (0) 1387 710286.

Printed in the United States
15834LVS00001B/136-147

9 781573 831888